W9-AWH-587

NATIONAL GALLERY OF ART

KRESS FOUNDATION STUDIES

IN THE HISTORY OF EUROPEAN ART

NUMBER TWO

FRENCH PAINTING IN THE TIME OF JEAN DE BERRY

THE LATE FOURTEENTH CENTURY AND THE PATRONAGE OF THE DUKE

BY MILLARD MEISS

PHAIDON

NATIONAL GALLERY OF ART : KRESS FOUNDATION
STUDIES IN THE HISTORY OF EUROPEAN ART

FRENCH PAINTING IN THE TIME OF JEAN DE BERRY

BY MILLARD MEISS

THE LATE FOURTEENTH CENTURY
AND THE PATRONAGE OF THE DUKE

PLATE VOLUME

PHAIDON

ALL RIGHTS RESERVED BY PHAIDON PRESS LTD · 5 CROMWELL PLACE · LONDON SW 7
FIRST PUBLISHED 1967
SECOND EDITION 1969

PHAIDON PUBLISHERS INC · NEW YORK
DISTRIBUTORS IN THE UNITED STATES: FREDERICK A. PRAEGER INC
III FOURTH AVENUE · NEW YORK · N.Y. 10003
LIBRARY OF CONGRESS CATALOG CARD NUMBER: 69–15047

SBN FOR COMPLETE SET OF TWO VOLUMES: 7148 1362 1
SBN FOR THIS VOLUME: 7148 1364 8

ILLUSTRATIONS ENGRAVED BY SCHWITTER A.G. · BASLE
AND PRINTED BY VSK PRINTERS · BASLE
BOUND BY A. W. BAIN AND CO LTD · LONDON · ENGLAND

MADE IN GREAT BRITAIN

ILLUSTRATIONS

The main manuscripts, to which entire chapters
are devoted, are reproduced first in the sequence of plates.
With rare exceptions the sequence of miniatures in the manuscripts is maintained.
Following these come the smaller or lesser manuscripts,
and from Fig. 287 onwards the comparative illustrations.
The sequence of reproductions of the *Très Belles Heures de Notre-Dame* (Figs. 6 to 50)
is that of the original manuscript as reconstructed by Durrieu.

1. Parement Master: *Crucifixion;*
at the sides *Church and Synagogue, Charles V and Jeanne de Bourbon* (reproduced opposite). Paris, Louvre.

3. Parement Master: *Flagellation.* Paris, Louvre.

2. Parement Master: *Betrayal.* Paris, Louvre.

5. Parement Master: *Entombment*. Paris, Louvre.

4. Parement Master: *Way to Calvary*. Paris, Louvre.

6. Parement Master and Workshop: *Annunciation; Virgin spinning, miraculously provided with food; Marriage of Virgin* (kneeling donor repainted). Paris, Bibl. nat., nouv. acq. lat. 3093, p. 2.

7. Parement Master and Workshop: *Visitation; Joseph questioning Virgin; Angel assuring Joseph; Virgin and Joseph at Bethlehem.*
Paris, Bibl. nat., nouv. acq. lat. 3093, p. 28.

8. Parement Master and Workshop: *Nativity; Annunciation to Shepherds*. Paris, Bibl. nat., nouv. acq. lat. 3093, p. 42.

9. Parement Master and Workshop: *Adoration of Magi; Annunciation to Magi; Magi before Herod.* Paris, Bibl. nat., nouv. acq. lat. 3093, p. 50.

10. Parement Master and Workshop: *Presentation in Temple; Virgin warned by angel; Miracle of the corn; Flight into Egypt.*
Paris, Bibl. nat., nouv. acq. lat. 3093, p. 56.

11. Parement Master and Workshop: *Christ among Doctors; Herod ordering Massacre of Innocents; Massacre of Innocents.*
Paris, Bibl. nat., nouv. acq. lat. 3093, p. 62.

12. Parement Master and Workshop: *Wedding at Cana; Christ blessing loaves and fishes; Eating of loaves and fishes.*
Paris, Bibl. nat., nouv. acq. lat. 3093, p. 68.

onuerte nos deus salutaris
noster.
Et auerte uam tuam a no
bis.

13. Parement Master and Workshop: *Coronation of Virgin; Assumption; Death of Virgin.*
Paris, Bibl. nat., nouv. acq. lat. 3093, p. 78.

14. Parement Master and Workshop: *Office of the Dead; Two Monks; Funeral Procession.* Paris, Bibl. nat., nouv. acq. lat. 3093, p. 104.

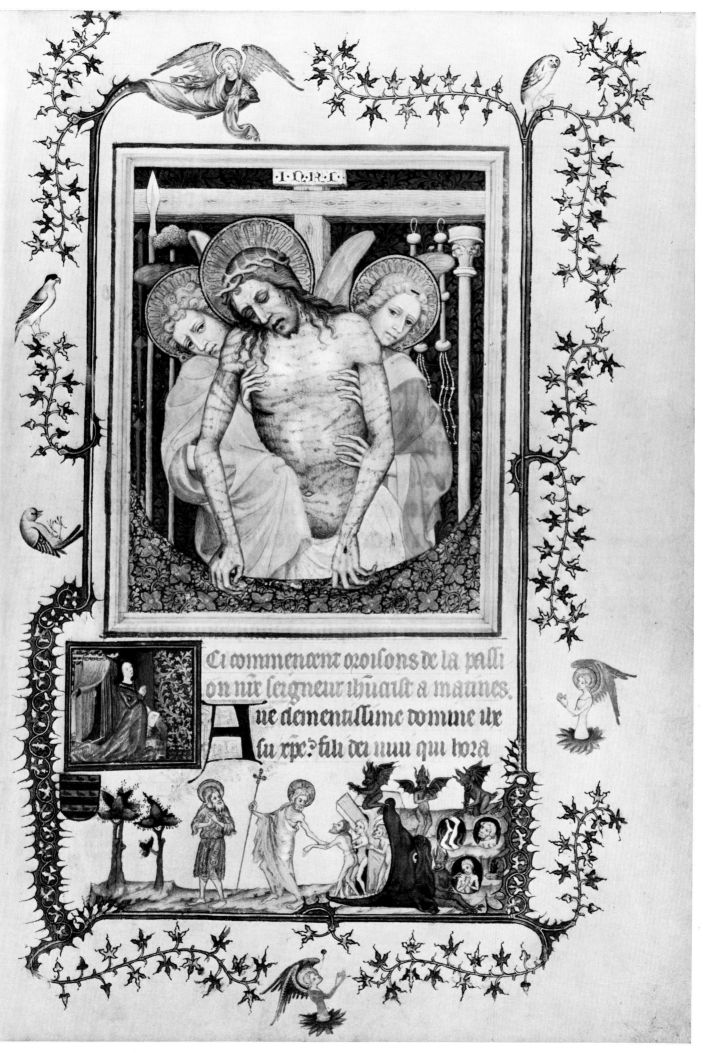

15. Parement Master and Workshop: *Man of Sorrows; Harrowing of Hell*. Paris, Bibl. nat., nouv. acq. lat. 3093, p. 155.

16. Parement Workshop, Baptist Master, and Holy Ghost Master: *Baptism; Holy Ghost and Virgin; Baptismal Procession*.
Paris, Bibl. nat., nouv. acq. lat. 3093, p. 162.

17. Parement Workshop and Holy Ghost Master: *Pentecost; Holy Ghost and Virgin; Sacrament of Baptism.*
Paris, Bibl. nat., nouv. acq. lat. 3093, p. 166.

18. Parement Workshop and Holy Ghost Master: *Resurrection of Dead; Holy Ghost and Virgin; Sacrament of Confirmation.*
Paris, Bibl. nat., nouv. acq. lat. 3093, p. 169.

19. Parement Workshop and Holy Ghost Master: *Descent of Holy Ghost on Faithful; Holy Ghost and Virgin; Sacrament of Eucharist.*
Paris, Bibl. nat., nouv. acq. lat. 3093, p. 173.

20. Parement Workshop and Holy Ghost Master: *Holy Ghost and Unbelievers; Holy Ghost and Virgin; Sacrament of Marriage.*
Paris, Bibl. nat., nouv. acq. lat. 3093, p. 176.

21. Parement Workshop and Holy Ghost Master: *Apostles going forth to preach; Holy Ghost and Virgin; Sacrament of Extreme Unction.*
Paris, Bibl. nat., nouv. acq. lat. 3093, p. 178.

22. Parement Master and Workshop: *Betrayal; Agony in Garden; Judas receiving pieces of silver*. Paris, Bibl. nat., nouv. acq. lat. 3093, p. 181.

Deus in adiutorium meum intende
Domine ad adiuuandum me
festina.
Gloria patri.

23. Parement Master and Workshop: *Christ before Caiaphas; Mocking; Christ before Annas.* Paris, Bibl. nat., nouv. acq. lat. 3093, p. 189.

24. Parement Master and Workshop: *Christ before Pilate; St. Peter and maid; Judas throwing away pieces of silver and hanging himself.*
Paris, Bibl. nat., nouv. acq. lat. 3093, p. 194.

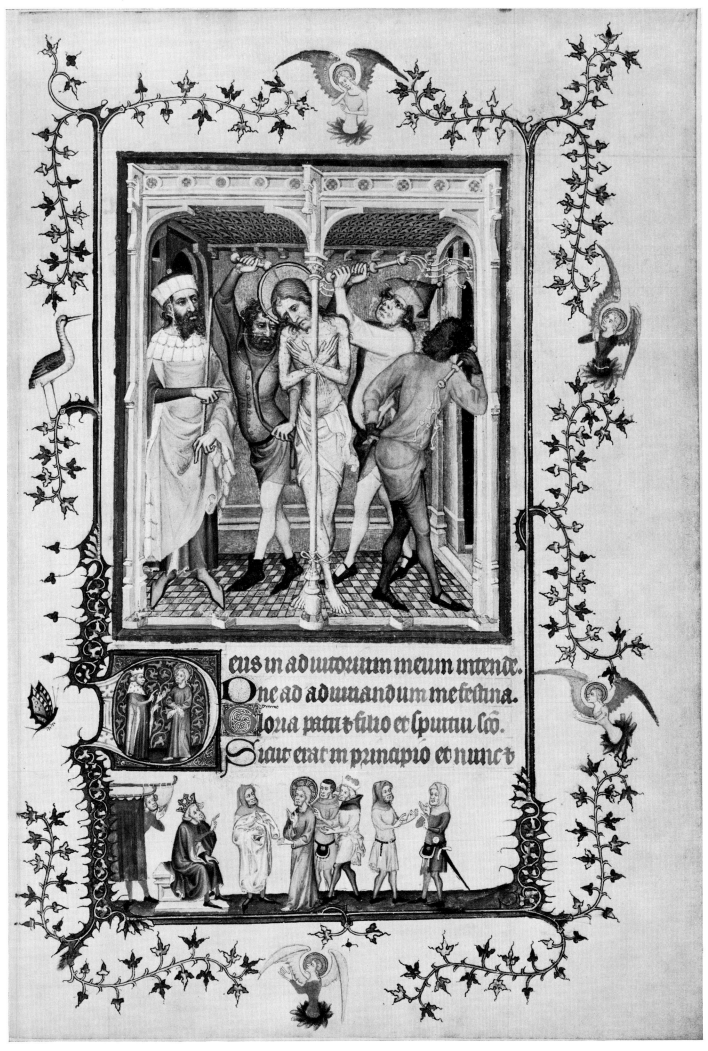

25. Parement Master and Workshop: *Flagellation; Christ before Pilate; Christ before Herod.*
Paris, Bibl. nat., nouv. acq. lat. 3093, p. 197.

26. Parement Workshop and Baptist Master: *Christ carrying Cross; Pilate washing hands; Ecce Homo.*
Paris, Bibl. nat., nouv. acq. lat. 3093, p. 203.

27. Parement Workshop and Baptist Master: *Crucifixion; Soldiers casting lots for garments; Christ nailed to Cross.*
Paris, Bibl. nat., nouv. acq. lat. 3093, p. 209.

28. Parement Workshop and Baptist Master: *Deposition; Joseph of Arimathea and Nicodemus before Pilate; Lamentation.*
Paris, Bibl. nat., nouv. acq. lat. 3093, p. 216.

29. Baptist Master: *St. John the Baptist in Desert*. Eyckian Painter: *St. John Preaching, Story of Salome.*
Heures de Turin, fol. 56 (burned).

30. Baptist Master: *Patriarchs, prophets and apostles.*
Heures de Turin, fol. 57v. (burned).

31. Baptist Master: *Mary Magdalene at Christ's feet
in house of Simon. Heures de Turin*, fol. 58 (burned).

32. Baptist Master: *Martyrs*. Paris, Louvre, Cabinet des Dessins.

33. Baptist Master: *Confessors.*
Paris, Louvre, Cabinet des Dessins.

34. Baptist Master: *Duke of Berry kneeling at prie-dieu
before enthroned Virgin. Heures de Turin*, fol. 78v. (burned).

35. Baptist Master: *St. Jerome at work aided by two clerks.
Heures de Turin*, fol. 80v. (burned).

36. Parement Workshop and Flemish painter:
God the Father Enthroned (damaged). Paris, Louvre, Cabinet des Dessins.

38. Parement Master and Workshop: *Christ in Glory*;
Two angel musicians; *Three angel musicians. Heures de Turin*, fol. 39v. (burned).

37. Parement Master and Workshop: *St. John the Evangelist and Virgin*;
Crucifixion; *Duke of Berry (?) presented to Christ*. Paris, Louvre, Cabinet des Dessins.

La messe de nr̃e dame q̃ len dit en lauēt:
Orate celi desuper et nubes pluant iu∫
tum aperiatur terra et germinet salua
torem. ps̃. Celi enarrant gloriam dei:

39. Baptist Master: *Annunciation*. Eyckian Painter: *Noah; Moses*. Turin, Museo Civico, *Heures de Milan*, fol. 1v.

Gaudeamus omnes in domino diem
festum celebrantes sub honore marie
virginis de cuius assumptione gaudent
angeli et collaudant filium dei. ps̃

40. Later Flemish painter over miniature from Parement Circle: *Coronation of the Virgin*. Eyckian Painter: *Virgin giving Girdle to Thomas; Death of the Virgin*. Turin, Museo Civico, *Heures de Milan*, fol. 100v.

41. Parement Workshop and Baptist Master: *Nativity*.
Turin, Museo Civico, *Heures de Milan*, fol. 4v.

42. Imitator of Parement Master: *Adoration of Magi*.
Turin, Museo Civico, *Heures de Milan*, fol. 13v.

43. Imitator of Parement Master: *Presentation in Temple*.
Turin, Museo Civico, *Heures de Milan*, fol. 16v.

44. Baptist Master: *Entry into Jerusalem*.
Turin, Museo Civico, *Heures de Milan*, fol. 20v.

45. Imitator of Parement Master: *Ascension.*
Turin, Museo Civico, *Heures de Milan*, fol. 80v.

46. Baptist Master: *Pentecost.*
Turin, Museo Civico, *Heures de Milan*, fol. 84v.

47. Baptist Master: *Institution of Eucharist.*
Turin, Museo Civico, *Heures de Milan*, fol. 90.

48. Baptist Master: *Martyrdom of St. Andrew.*
Turin, Museo Civico, *Heures de Milan*, fol. 122.

enedicta sit sancta trinitas atq indiui
sa unitas confitebimur ei quia fecit no
biscum misericordiam suam. ps. Be
nedicamus patrem et filium cum sanc

49. Parement Master and Workshop: *Trinity with Duke of Berry* (retouched); *Marriage; Ceremony of Marriage*.
Turin, Museo Civico, *Heures de Milan*, fol. 87.

50. Parement Master and Workshop: *Madonna with worshipper; Two angels; Christ preaching.*
Turin, Museo Civico, *Heures de Milan*, fol. 120.

Supp^t ft. n° 201

51. André Beauneveu: *Jeremiah*. Paris, Bibl. nat., fr. 13091, fol. 7v.

52. André Beauneveu: *St. Peter*. Paris, Bibl. nat., fr. 13091, fol. 8.

53. André Beauneveu: *David*. Paris, Bibl. nat., fr. 13091, fol. 9v.

t in ihcfum
rvistum filiu
cus umaun
dominum noftrum.

en ihcfu
crist son feul
fiz noftre
seigneur.

54. André Beauneveu: *St. Andrew*. Paris, Bibl. nat., fr. 13091, fol. 10.

55. André Beauneveu: *Isaiah*. Paris, Bibl. nat., fr. 13091, fol. 11v.

in conceptus
est de spiritu
sancto na-
tus ex maria uirgine.

vi est conceu
u du sami
espirit nes de
la vierge marie.

56. André Beauneveu: *St. James Major*. Paris, Bibl. nat., fr. 13091, fol. 12.

57. André Beauneveu: *Zachariah*. Paris, Bibl. nat., fr. 13091, fol. 13v.

58. André Beauneveu: *St. John the Evangelist*. Paris, Bibl. nat., fr. 13091, fol. 14.

59. André Beauneveu: *Hosea*. Paris, Bibl. nat., fr. 13091, fol. 15v.

escendit ad
infterna ter
cta die resur
rent a mortus.

escendit en
enfer le tiers
iour de mort

... resuscita.

60. André Beauneveu: *St. Thomas*. Paris, Bibl. nat., fr. 13091, fol. 16.

61. André Beauneveu: *Micah*. Paris, Bibl. nat., fr. 13091, fol. 17v.

62. André Beauneveu: *St. James Minor*. Paris, Bibl. nat., fr. 13091, fol. 18.

effundam de
spiritu meo
super omné
carnem.

ur tous ie
dommay de
mon es
prit.

63. André Beauneveu: *Joel*. Paris, Bibl. nat., fr. 13091, fol. 19v.

64. André Beauneveu: *St. Philip*. Paris, Bibl. nat., fr. 13091, fol. 20.

ccchm con
tra vos in
iudicio et
ero testis uelor.

ontre vous
en iugemēt
he seraip co
me tesmoign a yert.

65. André Beauneveu: *Zephaniah*. Paris, Bibl. nat., fr. 13091, fol. 21v.

66. André Beauneveu: *St. Bartholomew*. Paris, Bibl. nat., fr. 13091, fol. 22.

67. André Beauneveu: *Amos*. Paris, Bibl. nat., fr. 13091, fol. 23v.

anctam et   aintr eglile
cleliam ca   catholique
tholicam   dr fains la
fanctorum cõmunionē communium

68. André Beauneveu: *St. Matthew*. Paris, Bibl. nat., fr. 13091, fol. 24.

69. André Beauneveu: *Daniel*. Paris, Bibl. nat., fr. 13091, fol. 25v.

70. André Beauneveu: *St. Simon*. Paris, Bibl. nat., fr. 13091, fol. 26.

71. André Beauneveu: *Ezekiel*. Paris, Bibl. nat., fr. 13091, fol. 27v.

72. André Beauneveu: *St. Jude* (*Thaddeus*). Paris, Bibl. nat., fr. 13091, fol. 28.

73. André Beauneveu: *Malachi*. Paris, Bibl. nat., fr. 13091, fol. 29v.

74. André Beauneveu: *St. Matthias*. Paris, Bibl. nat., fr. 13091, fol. 30.

75. French illuminator: *David playing harp*.
Paris, Bibl. nat., fr. 13091, fol. 31.

76 and 77. Pseudo-Jacquemart and associate: *David pointing to his eyes. David pointing to his mouth*. Paris, Bibl. nat., fr. 13091, fols. 63 and 85.

78. Jacquemart de Hesdin: *Fool*. Paris, Bibl. nat., fr. 13091, fol. 106.

80. Pseudo–Jacquemart: *David playing carillon.* Paris, Bibl. nat., fr. 13091, fol. 153.

79. Jacquemart de Hesdin: *David saved from drowning.* Paris, Bibl. nat., fr. 13091, fol. 127.

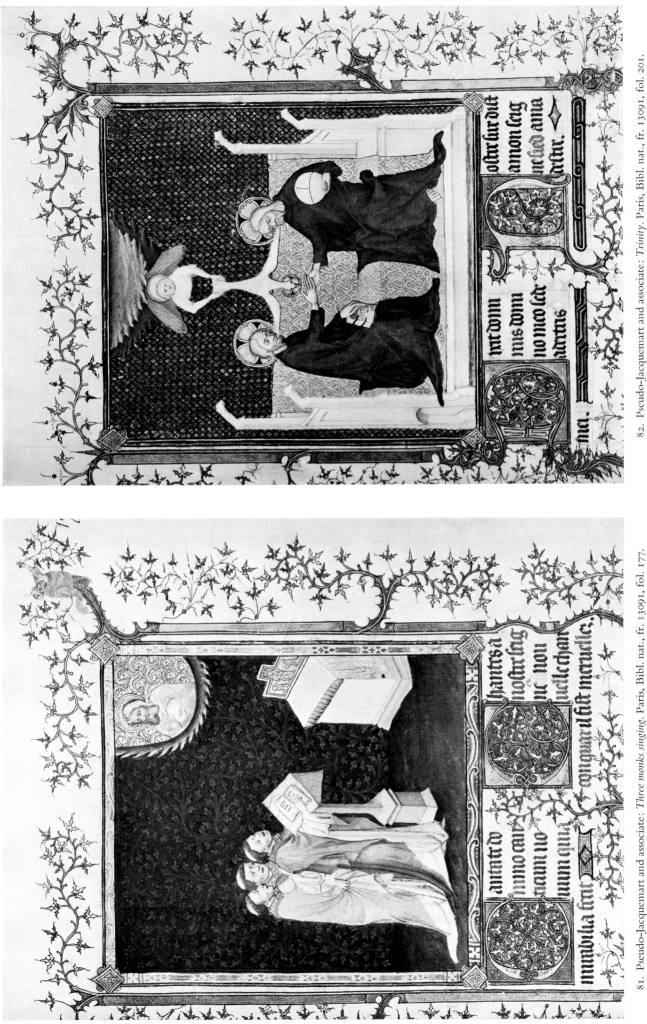

82. Pseudo-Jacquemart and associate: *Trinity*. Paris, Bibl. nat., fr. 13091, fol. 201.

81. Pseudo-Jacquemart and associate: *Three monks singing*. Paris, Bibl. nat., fr. 13091, fol. 177.

83. Pseudo-Jacquemart: *St. Paul Preaching; Fishes; David and St. Andrew (February)*. Paris, Bibl. nat., lat. 18014, fol. 1 v.

84. Pseudo-Jacquemart: *Isaiah and St. James Major (March)*. Paris, Bibl. nat., lat. 18014, fol. 2.

85. Pseudo-Jacquemart: *Zephaniah and St. Philip (June)*. Paris, Bibl. nat., lat. 18014, fol. 4.

86. Jacquemart and Pseudo-Jacquemart: *Dominican Friar Instructing Young Prince*.
Paris, Bibl. nat., lat. 18014, fol. 8.

87. Pseudo-Jacquemart: *Dominican Friar Instructing Young Prince*. Paris, Bibl. nat., lat. 18014, fol. 9v.

88. Pseudo-Jacquemart: *Christ and High Priest Eli; Death of Eli; Hophni and Phineas Sinning.*
Paris, Bibl. nat., lat. 18014, fol. 12.

89. Jacquemart: *Saint Louis, King of France, on His Deathbed.* Paris, Bibl. nat., lat. 18014, fol. 17.

90 and 91. Jacquemart: *Visitation. Nativity*. Paris, Bibl. nat., lat. 18014, fols. 32v and 38.

92. Passion Master and Jacquemart: *Annunciation to Shepherds*.
Paris, Bibl. nat., lat. 18014, fol. 40v.

93. Jacquemart: *Adoration of Magi*.
Paris, Bibl. nat., lat. 18014, fol. 42v.

94. Passion Master and Jacquemart: *Annunciation; Man of Sorrows with Virgin and St. John the Baptist; Duke of Berry; Twelve Apostles and Jeremiah.* Paris, Bibl. nat., lat. 18014, fol. 22.

95 and 96. Jacquemart and Trinity Master: *Flight into Egypt. Coronation of Virgin*. Paris, Bibl. nat., lat. 18014, fols. 45v and 48v.

97. Pseudo-Jacquemart: *Crucifixion*. Paris, Bibl. nat., lat. 18014, fol. 63v.

98. Trinity Master: *Baptism*. Paris, Bibl. nat., lat. 18014, fol. 67.

99. Passion Master: *Christ Enthroned and Four Evangelists*. Paris, Bibl. nat., lat. 18014, fol. 53.

100. Pseudo-Jacquemart: *Pentecost*. Paris, Bibl. nat., lat. 18014, fol. 69.

101. Trinity Master: *Trinity*. Paris, Bibl. nat., lat. 18014, fol. 70.

102. Pseudo-Jacquemart: *St. Peter Preaching*.
Paris, Bibl. nat., lat. 18014, fol. 71.

103. Trinity Master: *St. Peter Admitting Faithful into Church*.
Paris, Bibl. nat., lat. 18014, fol. 72.

104. Pseudo-Jacquemart: *SS. Peter and Paul Baptizing*.
Paris, Bibl. nat., lat. 18014, fol. 73.

105. Pseudo-Jacquemart: *St. Gregory Writing*.
Paris, Bibl. nat., lat. 18014, fol. 75.

106. Passion Master: *Betrayal*. Paris, Bibl. nat., lat. 18014, fol. 76.

107 and 108. Passion Master: *Christ before Pilate. Mocking*. Paris, Bibl. nat., lat. 18014, fols. 79v and 82.

109 and 110. Passion Master: *Flagellation. Christ Carrying Cross*. Paris, Bibl. nat., lat. 18014, fols. 83v and 86v.

111. Passion Master: *Crucifixion*. Paris, Bibl. nat., lat. 18014, fol. 89v.

112. Passion Master: *Deposition*. Paris, Bibl. nat., lat. 18014, fol. 92v.

113. Passion Master: *Entombment*. Paris, Bibl. nat., lat. 18014, fol. 94v.

114. Jacquemart: *Virgin and Child Adored by Jean de Berry*. Paris, Bibl. nat., lat. 18014, fol. 97v.

115. Trinity Master: *Berry* (?) *before the Lord.* – 116. Pseudo-Jacquemart and Trinity Master:
Virgin and Child Adored by a Prince (*Berry*). – 117. Pseudo-Jacquemart: *Berry* (?) *at Prayer.* Paris, Bibl. nat., lat. 18014, fols. 100v, 103v, 106.

118. Pseudo-Jacquemart: *Berry* (?) *before Christ.* – 119. Pseudo-Jacquemart: *Berry* (?) *and a Dominican before Christ.*
120. Pseudo-Jacquemart: *Berry* (?) *at Prayer.* Paris, Bibl. nat., lat. 18014, fols. 115v, 117v, 119.

121. Pseudo-Jacquemart: *Berry* (?), *the Madonna and St. John.* – 122. Pseudo-Jacquemart: *Berry* (?) *at Prayer.*
123. Pseudo-Jacquemart: *Berry* (?) *before the Madonna.* Paris, Bibl. nat., lat. 18014, fols. 120, 121v, 122.

124. Pseudo-Jacquemart: *Trinity*. – 125. Pseudo-Jacquemart: *Office of the Dead*.
126. Pseudo-Jacquemart: *Christ, Virgin, and Saints Enthroned in Paradise*. Paris, Bibl. nat., lat. 18014, fols. 132v, 134v, 136.

127. Trinity Master: *Trinity*. – 128. Pseudo-Jacquemart: *Berry (?) Attending Mass*.
129. Trinity Master: *Betrayal*. (retouched). Paris, Bibl. nat., lat. 18014, fols. 137v, 139, 140v.

130. Trinity Master: *Annunciation*. – 131. Pseudo-Jacquemart: *Nativity*.
132. Pseudo-Jacquemart: *Death of Virgin*. Paris, Bibl. nat., lat. 18014, fols. 141v, 143, 144.

133 and 134. Pseudo-Jacquemart: *Holy Confessors; Female Martyr Saints. Deposition; Resurrection.* Paris, Bibl. nat., lat. 18014, fols. 105v and 141.

135 and 136. Pseudo-Jacquemart: *Virgin and Her Parents Entering Temple; Virgin at Prayer. Virgin Nursing Child; Annunciation of Virgin's Death.*
Paris, Bibl. nat., lat. 18014, fols. 142v and 143v.

137. Pseudo-Jacquemart (?): *Berry (?) at Prayer.* – 138. Pseudo-Jacquemart: *Entombment of Christ.*
139. Trinity Master: *Agony in Garden.* Paris, Bibl. nat., lat. 18014, fols. 145v, 155, 158.

140. Fifth Master: *Way to Calvary.* – 141. Fifth Master: *Erection of Cross.*
142. Pseudo-Jacquemart: *Christ Nailed to Cross.* Paris, Bibl. nat., lat. 18014, fols. 160, 161, 162.

143. Trinity Master: *Holy Women at Sepulcher.* – 144. Pseudo-Jacquemart: *Crucifixion.*
145. Pseudo-Jacquemart: *Harrowing of Hell.* Paris, Bibl. nat., lat. 18014, fols. 163, 164, 166.

146. Pseudo-Jacquemart: *Berry* (?) *at Prayer*. – 147. Pseudo-Jacquemart: *Berry* (?) *at Mass*.
148. Pseudo-Jacquemart: *Berry* (?) *Receiving the Wafer during Mass*. Paris, Bibl. nat., lat. 18014, fols. 167v, 172, 173v.

149. Pseudo-Jacquemart: *Communion*. – 150. Pseudo-Jacquemart: *Berry* (?) *at Prayer*.
151. Pseudo-Jacquemart: *Christ, St. Martha and St. Julian on Voyage*. Paris, Bibl. nat., lat. 18014, fols. 174v, 176v, 181v.

152 and 153. Trinity Master: *Abraham Adoring Trinity. Christ Enthroned between Seraphim*.
Paris, Bibl. nat., lat. 18014, fols. 188 and 189.

154. Trinity Master: *Trinity*. Paris, Bibl. nat., lat. 18014, fol. 183.

155. Pseudo-Jacquemart: *Baptism*. – 156. Trinity Master: *Christ on Mount Tabor*.
157. Pseudo-Jacquemart: *Christ Preaching*. Paris, Bibl. nat., lat. 18014, fols. 191, 192, 193.

158. Trinity Master: *Trinity*. – 159. Pseudo-Jacquemart: *Berry (?) before Christ on the Cross*.
160. Pseudo-Jacquemart: *Pentecost*. Paris, Bibl. nat., lat. 18014, fols. 196, 196v, 197v.

161. Pseudo-Jacquemart: *Berry (?) before the Trinity*. – 162. Trinity Master: *Berry before the Madonna Enthroned*.
163. Fifth Master: *Berry (?) Led by an Angel*. Paris, Bibl. nat., lat. 18014, fols. 198, 198v, 199v.

164. Trinity Master and Pseudo-Jacquemart: *Annunciation to Zacharias*.
Paris, Bibl. nat., lat. 18014, fol. 203.

165. Pseudo-Jacquemart: *Visitation*.
Paris, Bibl. nat., lat. 18014, fol. 206.

166. Passion Master and Trinity Master: *Birth of St. John the Baptist
and Zacharias Writing Name*. Paris, Bibl. nat., lat. 18014, fol. 207.

167. Passion Master: *St. John the Baptist in Desert*.
Paris, Bibl. nat., lat. 18014, fol. 208.

168. Jacquemart and Trinity Master: *Baptism of Christ*.
Paris, Bibl. nat., lat. 18014, fol. 209v.

169. Jacquemart and Trinity Master: *St. John the Baptist before Herod*.
Paris, Bibl. nat., lat. 18014, fol. 211.

170. Passion Master and Trinity Master: *Salome's Dance*.
Paris, Bibl. nat., lat. 18014, fol. 212v.

171. Jacquemart, Trinity Master, and Pseudo-Jacquemart:
Salome and the Executioner. Paris, Bibl. nat., lat. 18014, fol. 214.

172 and 173. Pseudo-Jacquemart: *Crucifixion. Solomon's Throne.* Paris, Bibl. nat., lat. 18014, fols. 239 and 278v.

174 and 175. Pseudo-Jacquemart: *Three Living and Three Dead. Lamentation.* Paris, Bibl. nat., lat. 18014, fols. 282 and 286.

176. Pseudo-Jacquemart: *Office of the Dead*. Paris, Bibl. nat., lat. 18014, fol. 217.

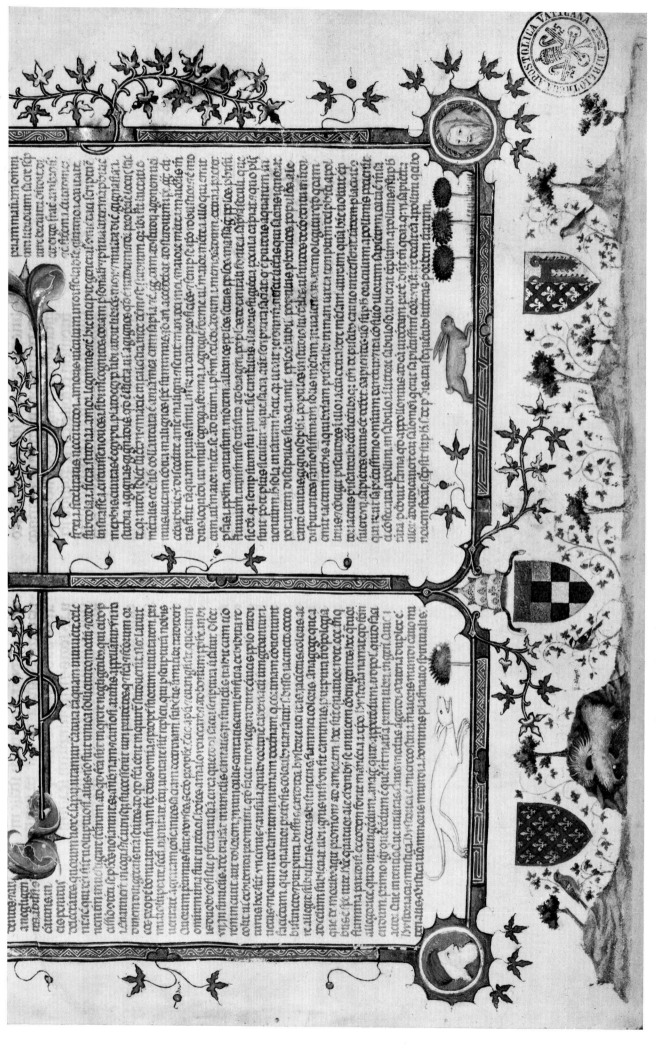

177. Jacquemart de Hesdin, 1389–94: *Frieze in lower border*. Rome, Bibl. Vaticana, lat. 50, fol. 1.

178. Jacquemart and the Trinity Master, 1389–94: *Heraldic devices, emblems, birds and butterflies*. Rome, Bibl. Vaticana, lat. 51, fol. 1.

179. French painter, *ca.* 1390: *Jean de Berry Kneeling between SS. Andrew and John the Baptist.* Brussels, Bibl. Royale, ms. 11060–1, p. 10.

180. French painter, *ca.* 1390: *Virgin and Child*. Brussels, Bibl. Royale, ms. 11060–1, p. 11.

181. Jacquemart: *Jean de Berry with SS. Andrew and John the Baptist before the Virgin*. Brussels, Bibl. Royale, ms. 11060–1, p. 14 (detail).

8.

182. Jacquemart: *Annunciation*. Brussels, Bibl. Royale, ms. 11060–1, p. 18.

183. Jacquemart: *Visitation*. Brussels, Bibl. Royale, ms. 11060–1, p. 54.

184. Jacquemart: *Nativity*. Brussels, Bibl. Royale, ms. 11060–1, p. 72.

185. Jacquemart: *Annunciation to the Shepherds*. Brussels, Bibl. Royale, ms. 11060–1, p. 82 (detail).

186. Jacquemart: *Adoration of the Magi*. Brussels, Bibl. Royale, ms. 11060–1, p. 90.

187. Jacquemart: *Presentation in the Temple*. Brussels, Bibl. Royale, ms. 11060–1, p. 98.

188. Jacquemart: *Flight into Egypt*. Brussels, Bibl. Royale, ms. 11060–1, p. 106 (detail).

189. Jacquemart and assistant: *Coronation of the Virgin*. Brussels, Bibl. Royale, ms. 11060–1, p. 118.

190. Jacquemart and assistant: *Christ in Majesty*. Brussels, Bibl. Royale, ms. 11060–1, p. 130.

191. Jacquemart and assistant: *Betrayal*. Brussels, Bibl. Royale, ms. 11060–1, p. 164.

192. Jacquemart and assistant: *Christ before Pilate*. Brussels, Bibl. Royale, ms. 11060–1, p. 168.

193. Jacquemart and assistant: *Flagellation*. Brussels, Bibl. Royale, ms. 11060–1, p. 182.

194. Jacquemart and assistant: *Christ Carrying the Cross*. Brussels, Bibl. Royale, ms. 11060–1, p. 186.

195. Jacquemart and assistant: *Crucifixion*. Brussels, Bibl. Royale, ms. 11060–1, p. 190.

196. Jacquemart and assistant: *Deposition*. Brussels, Bibl. Royale, ms. 11060–1, p. 194 (detail).

197. Jacquemart and assistant: *Entombment*. Brussels, Bibl. Royale, ms. 11060–1, p. 198.

198. Jacquemart: *Office of the Dead*. Brussels, Bibl. Royale, ms. 11060–1, p. 202.

199. Brussels Initials Master: *Lamentation*. Brussels, Bibl. Royale, ms. 11060-1, p. 195.

200 and 201. Brussels Initials Master: *Isaiah. Jeremiah.* Brussels, Bibl. Royale, ms. 11060–1, pp. 19 and 55.

202 and 203. Brussels Initials Master: *Moses and the Burning Bush. Augustus and Sibyl.* Brussels, Bibl. Royale, ms. 11060–1, pp. 73 and 83.

204 and 205. Brussels Initials Master: *Solomon and Queen of Sheba. Samuel Brought to Eli*. Brussels, Bibl. Royale, ms. 11060–1, pp. 91 and 99.

206 and 207. Brussels Initials Master: *Daniel and the Vision of the Broken Statue. Assumption of Virgin*. Brussels, Bibl. Royale, ms. 11060–1, pp. 107 and 119.

208 and 209. Brussels Initials Master: *David Repenting. Christ Led into Pretorium.* Brussels, Bibl. Royale, ms. 11060–1, pp. 131 and 165.

210 and 211. Brussels Initials Master: *Mocking of Christ. Christ Crowned with Thorns.* Brussels, Bibl. Royale, ms. 11060–1, pp. 169 and 183.

212 and 213. Brussels Initials Master: *Christ Nailed to Cross. Two Jews before Pilate.* Brussels, Bibl. Royale, ms. 11060–1, pp. 187 and 191.

214 and 215. Brussels Initials Master: *Harrowing of Hell. Office of the Dead.* Brussels, Bibl. Royale, ms. 11060–1, pp. 199 and 203.

216. Pseudo-Jacquemart: *Lamentation*. Paris, Bibl. nat., lat. 919, fol. 77.

218. Pseudo-Jacquemart and Egerton Workshop: *December. St. Paul preaching; Goat; Daniel and St. Matthias*. Paris, Bibl. nat., lat. 919, fol. 6v.

219. Pseudo-Jacquemart: *Joachim's offering rejected; Duke of Berry adoring Virgin and Child.* Paris, Bibl. nat., lat. 919, fol. 8.

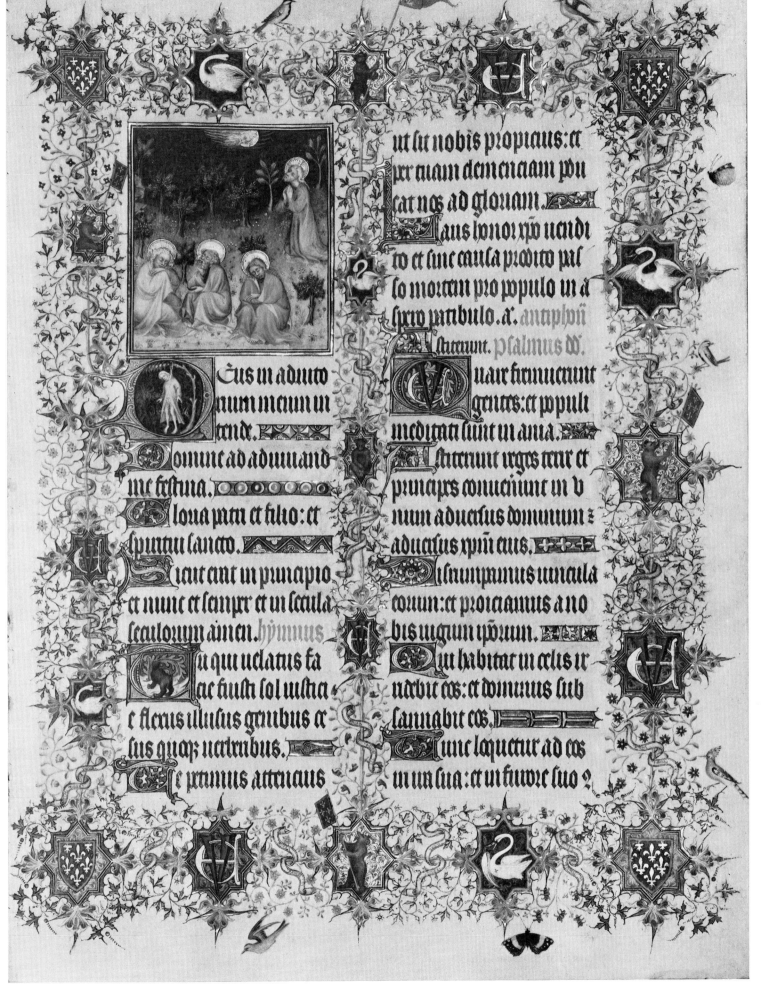

220. Pseudo-Jacquemart: *Agony in Garden; Judas hanging himself*. Paris, Bibl. nat., lat. 919, fol. 65.

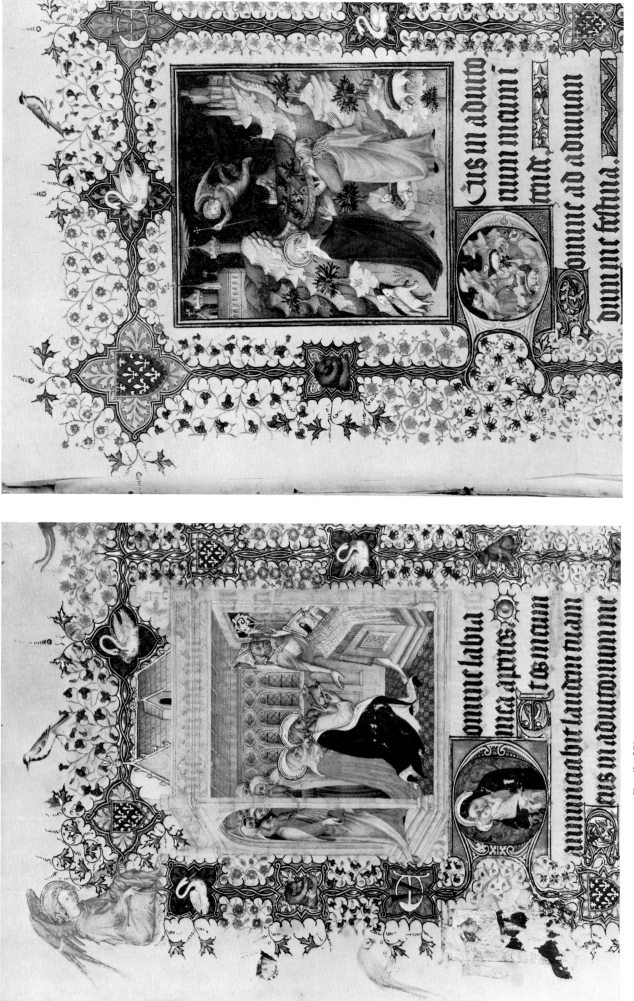

222. Pseudo-Jacquemart: *Annunciation to Joachim and Anna*; *Annunciation to Shepherds.*
Paris, Bibl. nat., lat. 919, fol. 18.

221. Detail of Fig. 219.

224. Pseudo-Jacquemart: *Presentation of Virgin*; *Anna leading Virgin*. Paris, Bibl. nat., lat. 919, fol. 31.

223. Pseudo-Jacquemart: *Birth of Virgin*; *Anna nursing Virgin*. Paris, Bibl. nat., lat. 919, fol. 28.

226. Pseudo-Jacquemart: *Entry into Jerusalem; Christ blessing people.*
Paris, Bibl. nat., lat. 919, fol. 61.

225. Pseudo-Jacquemart: *Marriage of Virgin.* Boucicaut Workshop: *Joachim, Anna and Virgin.*
Paris, Bibl. nat., lat. 919, fol. 37.

228. Pseudo-Jacquemart and assistants: *Resurrection*; *Holy Women at Sepulcher*. Paris, Bibl. nat., lat. 919, fol. 81.

227. Pseudo-Jacquemart: *Lamentation*. Paris, Bibl. nat., lat. 919, fol. 77.

229. Pseudo-Jacquemart and assistants: *Baptism; Lamb of God*. Paris, Bibl. nat., lat. 919, fol. 86.

230. Assistant of Pseudo-Jacquemart and Boucicaut Workshop: *Trinity; St. Augustine and Christ Child.* Paris, Bibl. nat., lat. 919, fol. 93.

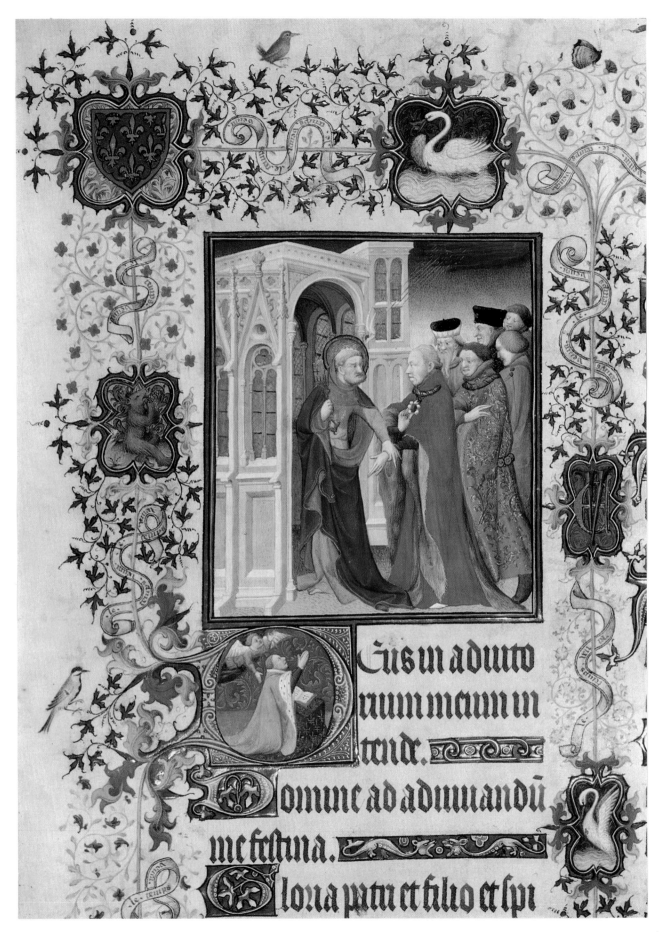

231. Bedford Master and associate: *Jean de Berry and Companions before St. Peter; Berry at Prayer.* Paris, Bibl. nat., lat. 919, fol. 96.

232. Pseudo-Jacquemart: *Office of the Dead; Monk reading*. Paris, Bibl. nat., lat. 919, fol. 106.

233 and 234. Pseudo-Jacquemart: *Meeting at Golden Gate; Joachim and Anna. Virgin in Temple; Berry at Prayer.*
Paris, Bibl. nat., lat. 919, fols. 24 and 34.

235 and 236. Pseudo-Jacquemart: *Wedding at Cana; Distribution of remaining food among poor. Crucifixion; Man of Sorrows.*
Paris, Bibl. nat., lat. 919, fols. 41 and 53.

237 and 238. Assistant of Pseudo-Jacquemart: *Pentecost; Trinity. Judas receiving pieces of silver; Judas throwing away pieces of silver.*
Paris, Bibl. nat., lat. 919, fols. 56 and 67.

239. Workshops of Pseudo-Jacquemart and of Boucicaut Master: *Spoliation; Mocking.* – 240. Follower of Boucicaut Master
and Pseudo-Jacquemart: *Christ attached to Cross; Soldiers casting lots for garments.* Paris, Bibl. nat., lat. 919, fols. 70 and 74.

241. Followers of Pseudo-Jacquemart and of Boucicaut Master: *Pentecost; Angel giving food to Virgin.* – 242. Follower of Pseudo-Jacquemart: *St. Peter preaching; Dove of Holy Ghost.* Paris, Bibl. nat., lat. 919, fols. 89 and 94.

243 and 244. Followers of Pseudo-Jacquemart and of Boucicaut Master: *SS. Peter and Paul baptizing; Duke of Berry at prayer. St. Peter celebrating Mass; Berry at Prayer.* Paris, Bibl. nat., lat. 919, fols. 97 and 98.

245. Pseudo-Jacquemart: *Annunciation*. – 246. Pseudo-Jacquemart (Workshop): *Joachim and Anna*.
Paris, Coll. Comte Jean Durrieu, Prayer Book.

247. Pseudo-Jacquemart: *Birth of the Virgin*. Paris, Coll. Comte Jean Durrieu, Prayer Book. – 248. Pseudo-Jacquemart: Initial.
London, Brit. Mus., Harley 4947, fol. 2.

249. Pseudo-Jacquemart: *Isaiah and St. James Major* (detail of *March*). Paris, Bibl. nat., lat. 919, fol. 2.

250. Pucelle: Line-ending. New York,
The Cloisters, *Heures de Jeanne d'Évreux*, fol. 160.

251. Pseudo-Jacquemart: Line-ending.
Paris, Bibl. nat., lat. 919, fol. 112.

252. Paris, Bibl. nat., lat. 919, fol. 64, showing gray turret and traces of double gray lines.

253. Pseudo-Jacquemart: *Four Evangelists.*
Bourges, Bibl. municipale, ms. 48, fol. 1.

254. Pseudo-Jacquemart: *Coronation by the Trinity.*
Bourges, Bibl. municipale, ms. 34, fol. 1v.

255 and 256. Pseudo-Jacquemart: *Annunciation. Madonna and Writing Child.* Leningrad, State Library, ms. Q.v.I.8.

257 and 258. Pseudo-Jacquemart: *Visitation. Annunciation to the Shepherds.* London, Brit. Mus., Add. 32454, fols. 22 and 32.

259. French: *Nativity*.
Leningrad, State Library, ms. Q.v.I.8.

260. Pucelle Workshop: *Suicide of Judas*.
Paris, Bibl. nat., lat. 10484, fol. 12v.

261. The Limbourgs: *Way to Calvary*.
New York, The Cloisters, *Belles Heures*, fol. 138v.

262. French: *Annunciation to the Shepherds*.
Baltimore, Walters Art Gallery, ms. 287, fol. 70.

263. Workshop of Jacquemart: *Entry into Jerusalem*. London, Brit. Mus., Yates Thompson 37, fol. 159.

264. Trinity Master: *Crucifixion*. London, Brit. Mus., Yates Thompson 37, fol. 118v.

265. Pseudo-Jacquemart Workshop: *Visitation*.
London, Brit. Mus., Yates Thompson 37, fol. 36v.

266. Workshop of Baptist Master: *Pentecost*.
London, Brit. Mus., Yates Thompson 37, fol. 122.

267. Luçon Workshop: *Adoration of the Magi*.
London, Brit. Mus., Yates Thompson 37, fol. 58.

268. Luçon Master: *Birth of Baptist*.
Paris, Bibl. nat., lat. 8886, fol. 413.

269. Humility Master: *Madonna of Humility*.
London, Brit. Mus., Yates Thompson 37, fol. 92.

270. Humility Master: *Madonna of Humility*.
London, Brit. Mus., Harley 2952, fol. 71v.

271 and 272. Humility Master: *Trinity*. *Saints*. London, Brit. Mus., Yates Thompson 37, fols. 79 and 86.

273. Humility Master: *Madonna of Humility*.
London, Brit. Mus., Harley 2952, fol. 86v.

274. Humility Master: *Madonna of Humility*.
London, Brit. Mus., Harley 2952, fol. 115.

275. Humility Master: *Flight into Egypt*.
London, Brit. Mus., Harley 2952, fol. 156.

276. Pseudo-Jacquemart: *Annunciation*.
London, Brit. Mus., Yates Thompson 37, fol. 19.

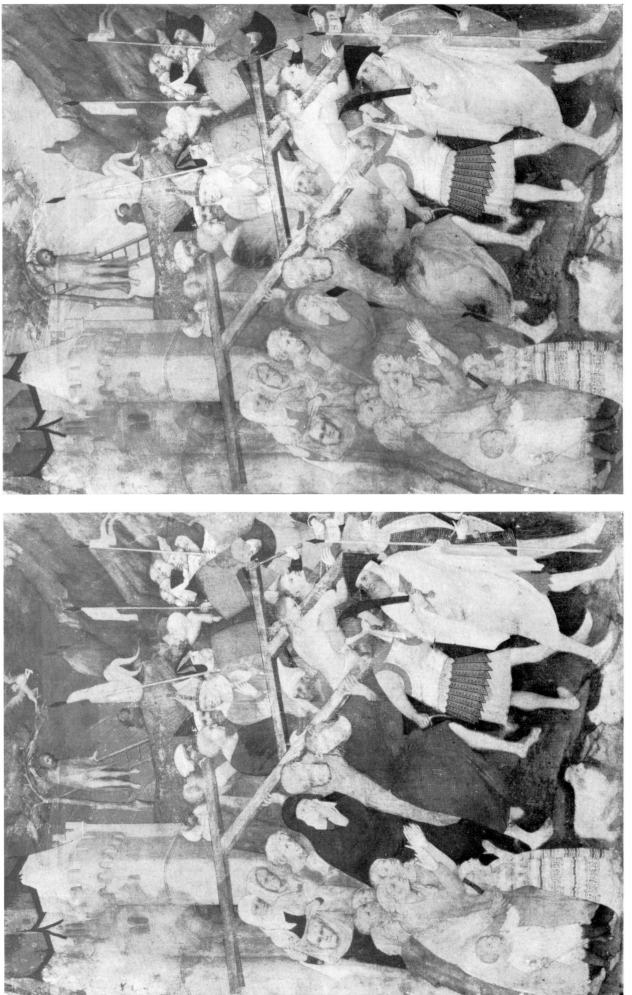

278. Jacquemart: *Way to Calvary*. Paris, Louvre (infra-red).

277. Jacquemart: *Way to Calvary*. Paris, Louvre.

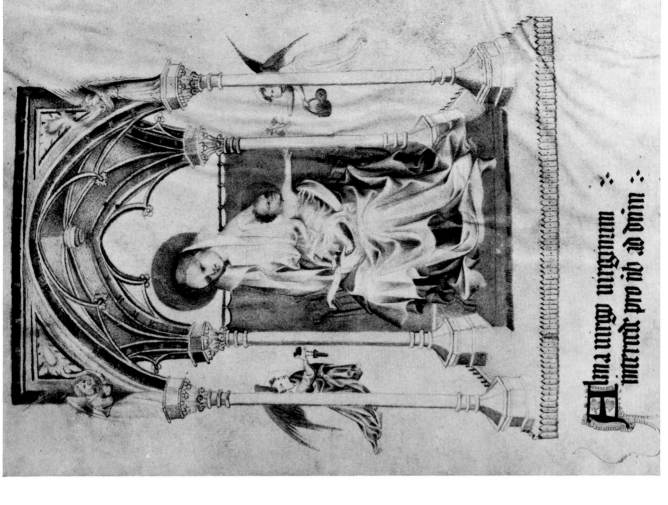

280. French, *ca.* 1400 (after Jacquemart): *Madonna with the writing Child and Angels.* Barcelona, S. María del Mar (destroyed or lost).

279. Jacquemart (?): *Madonna.*
New York, Morgan Library, M. 346, verso of cover.

281–283. Jacquemart (?): New York, Morgan Library, M. 346, fols. 1, 1 v (retouched), and 2v.

284–286. Jacquemart and predecessor (?): New York, Morgan Library, M. 346, fols. 3, 3v and 4v.

COMPARATIVE
ILLUSTRATIONS

287. French, 1401–2: *Marcia Painting a Self-Portrait*. Paris, Bibl. nat., fr. 12420, fol. 101 v. – 288. German, 1473: *Marcia Painting*. Woodcut in *Von Etlichen Frauen*, Ulm. – 289. Master of Berry's Cleres Femmes, before 1404: *Marcia Painting a Self-Portrait*. Paris, Bibl. nat., fr. 598, fol. 100v.

290. French, 1401–2: *Thamar Paints a Madonna*. Paris, Bibl. nat., fr. 12420, fol. 86.
291. Master of Berry's Cleres Femmes, before 1404: *Thamar Paints a Madonna*. Paris, Bibl. nat., fr. 598, fol. 86.

292. French, 1401–2: *Irene Coloring a Madonna*. Paris, Bibl. nat., fr. 12420, fol. 92v. – 293. Venetian, 1506: *Irene Declaiming*. Woodcut in *De claris mulieribus*, Tridinus, Venice. – 294. Master of Berry's Cleres Femmes, before 1404: *Irene Paints a Holy Face*. Paris, Bibl. nat., fr. 598, fol. 92.

295. Tommaso da Modena, 1352: *Nicholas of Rouen with Magnifying Glass*. Treviso, S. Niccolò. – 296. French (?), *ca.* 1420: *St. Matthew*. Milan, Bibl. Trivulziana, ms. 445, fol. 15. – 297. French, *ca.* 1400: *St. Luke*. New York, Morgan Library, ms. 331, fol. 187.

298. French, *ca.* 1365–80: *Story of Jacob*. Paris, Bibl. nat., fr. 15397, fol. 47v.

299. French: *Philotis and Syra* (*Hecyra*). Paris, Bibl. nat., lat. 8193, fol. 128v.　　300. French: *Demea and Micio* (*Adelphoe*). Paris, Bibl. nat., lat. 8193, fol. 118

301. Bondol (?): *Abraham and the Three Angels*. Paris, Bibl. nat., fr. 15397, fol. 26.

302. Neapolitan, 1362: *Samson and the Lion*. Rome, Bibl. Vaticana, lat. 3550, fol. 128.
303. Florentine, 1427: *Andrevuola and Gabriotto*. Paris, Bibl. nat., ital. 63, p. 150.

304 and 305. Boucicaut Workshop: *Marriage of Philippe le Hardi and Marguerite de Flandre*.
London, Brit. Mus., Cotton Nero E II, Vol. II, fol. 217 and drawing.

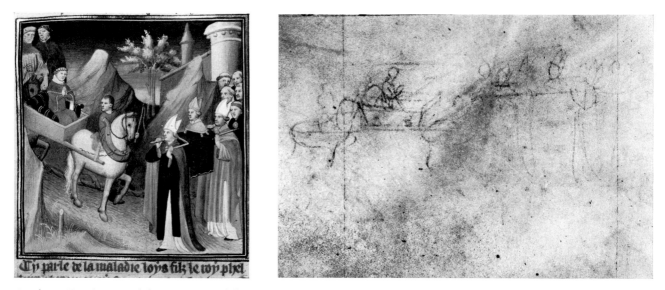

306 and 307. Boucicaut Workshop: *Messengers before King Louis*. London, Brit. Mus., Cotton Nero E II, Vol. II, fol. 45 and drawing.

308 and 309. Boucicaut Workshop: *King Louis before Reliquary of St. Denis*. London, Brit. Mus., Cotton Nero E II, Vol. II, fol. 4v and drawing.

310 and 311. Boucicaut Workshop: *Louis IX venerates a Reliquary*. London, Brit. Mus., Cotton Nero E II, Vol. II, fol. 36 and drawing.

312 and 313. French, *ca.* 1411: *Abraham and the Three Angels.* London, Brit. Mus., Royal 19 D III, Vol. I, fol. 20 and drawing.

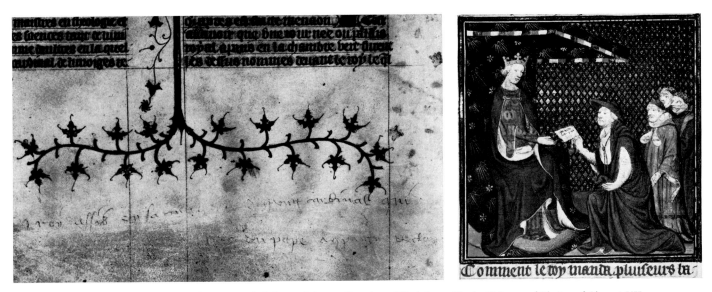

314 and 315. Inscription in lower margin below miniature. Boucicaut Workshop: *Charles V Learns of Election of Clement VII.*
London, Brit. Mus., Cotton Nero E II, Vol. II, fol. 238v.

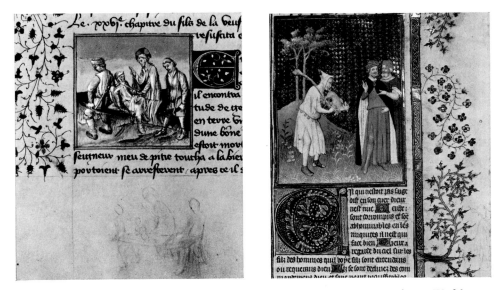

316. French, *ca.* 1420: *Christ Resurrects the Widow's Son.* London, Brit. Mus., Royal 20 B IV, fol. 61v.
317. Boucicaut Workshop: *The Fool Mocked.* London, Brit. Mus., Royal 15 D III, fol. 262.

318. Cité des Dames Workshop: *God as Beginner and as Master Painter*. Rome, Bibl. Vaticana, Palat. lat. 1989, fol. 189v.

319. Cité des Dames Workshop: *Androlla and Gabriel*. Rome, Bibl. Vaticana, Palat. lat. 1989, fol. 136.

320. Flemish Master, *ca.* 1440: *Androlla and Gabriel*. Paris, Bibl. de l'Arsenal, ms. 5070, fol. 164v.

321. Cité des Dames Workshop: *Richard and Catelle*. Rome, Bibl. Vaticana, Palat. lat. 1989, fol. 97.

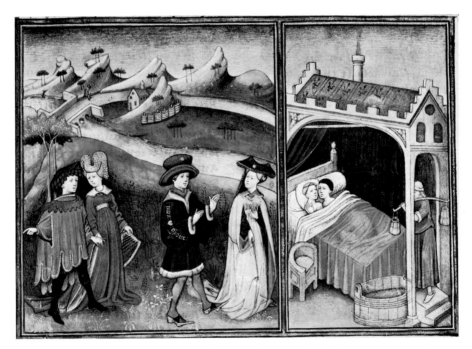

322. Master of Guillebert de Mets: *Richard and Catelle*. Paris, Bibl. de l'Arsenal, ms. 5070, fol. 116.

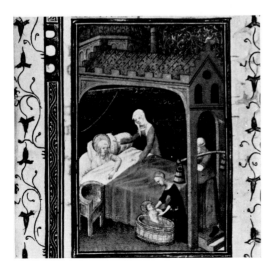

323. Egerton Workshop: *Birth of the Virgin*.
London, Brit. Mus., Harley 2897, fol. 385.

324. Egerton Workshop: *Christine and the Noblemen*.
Paris, Bibl. nat., fr. 836, fol. 65.

325. Cité des Dames Workshop: *God Carrying Adam.*
Paris, Bibl. nat., fr. 9, fol. 8.

326. French, *ca.* 1400: *Man of Sorrows.* Florence, Palazzo Pitti.

327. Rohan Workshop: *Vesperbild.*
Paris, Bibl. nat., lat. 9471, fol. 41.

328. Neapolitan: *Massacre of the Innocents* (detail).
Paris, Bibl. nat., fr. 9561, fol. 138.

329. French, *ca.* 1425: *Nativity*. London, Brit. Mus., Add. 18192, fol. 52. – 330. Amiens, late 13th century: *Nativity*.
New York, Morgan Library, ms. 729, fol. 246v. – 331. Vitale da Bologna: *Nativity* (detail). Bologna, Pinacoteca (from Mezzaratta).

332. Rohan Workshop: *Nativity*.
Paris, Bibl. nat., lat. 1156A, fol. 48.

333. Master of Flémalle: *Madonna at the Fireplace*.
Leningrad, Hermitage.

334. Luçon Master, 1401: *"Fons Vitae."*
Barcelona, Bibl. Central, ms. 1850, fol. 172.

335 and 336. Pucelle: *Annunciation. Crucifixion*. New York, The Cloisters, *Heures de Jeanne d'Évreux*, fols. 16 and 68v.

337 and 338. Pucelle: *Presentation in the Temple. Annunciation to the Shepherds.*
New York, The Cloisters, *Heures de Jeanne d'Évreux*, fols. 76 and 62.

339. Duccio: *Crucifixion*. Siena, Opera del Duomo.

340. Associate of Pucelle: *Siege of a Castle*. Paris, Bibl. nat., nouv. acq. fr. 24541, fol. 70v. – 341. Associate of Pucelle: *All Saints*, *Heures de Jeanne de Navarre*, fol. 81v. Whereabouts unknown.

342. Pucelle: *Entombment*. New York, The Cloisters, *Heures de Jeanne d'Évreux*, fol. 82v.
343. Workshop of Pucelle: *Death of the Virgin*. Chantilly, Musée Condé, ms. 51, fol. 322.

344. Pucelle and Workshop: *David and Goliath; Despair; Extreme Unction; Hope*. Paris, Bibl. nat., lat. 10483, fol. 17v.

345 and 346. Associate of Pucelle: *Annunciation. Nativity. Heures de Jeanne de Navarre*, fols. 39 and 50. Whereabouts unknown.

347. Associate of Pucelle: *Queen Jeanne gives alms.* – 348. Pucelle Workshop: *Mockery. Heures de Jeanne de Navarre*, fols. 123v and 110. Whereabouts unknown.

349. Workshop of Pucelle: *Christ in Majesty.* Geneva, Bibl. publique et universitaire, fr. 2, fol. 1.

350. Associate of Pucelle: *Flight into Egypt. Heures de Jeanne de Navarre*, fol. 61. Whereabouts unknown.
351. The Passion Master: *Trinity*. Paris, Bibl. nat., lat. 1052, fol. 154.

352. Pucelle Workshop: *Betrayal*. – 353. Pucelle: *Dixit Insipiens*. Geneva, Bodmer Library, *Psalter of Bonne de Luxembourg*, fols. 246 and 83.

354 and 355. Pucelle: *The Quick and the Dead*. Geneva, Bodmer Library, *Psalter of Bonne de Luxembourg*, fols. 320v and 321.

356. Workshop of Pucelle: *Stigmatization of St. Francis*. Rome, Bibl. Vaticana, Urb. lat. 603, fol. 466v. – 357. Workshop of Pucelle: *John the Evangelist Writing*. Paris, Bibl. nat., lat. 11935, fol. 634. – 358. Workshop of Pucelle: *The Prophecy of Obadiah*. Chantilly, Musée Condé, ms. 51, fol. 212v.

359. The Passion Master: *Nativity*. Paris, Bibl. nat., lat. 1052, fol. 28v. – 360. Pucelle: *February*. New York, The Cloisters, *Heures de Jeanne d'Évreux*.

361. Pucelle: *David and Goliath*. Geneva, Bodmer Library, *Psalter of Bonne de Luxembourg*, fol. 15. – 362. The Passion Master: *David and Goliath*. Paris, Bibl. nat., lat. 1052, fol. 217.

363. Workshop of Pucelle and the Passion Master: *Visitation*. – 364. Passion Master: *Annunciation to the Shepherds* and *Way to Calvary*. London, Brit. Mus., Yates Thompson 27, fols. 44v and 70v.

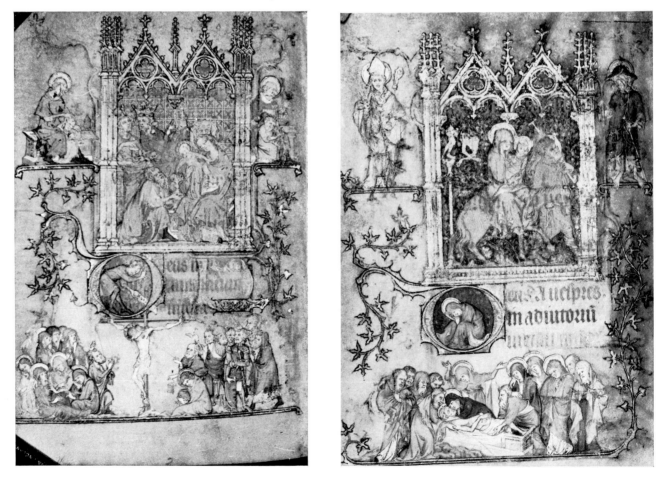

365. Pucelle Workshop (Passion Master): *Adoration of the Magi* and *Crucifixion*. – 366. Pucelle and the Passion Master: *Flight into Egypt* and *Entombment*. London, Brit. Mus., Yates Thompson 27, fols. 74v and 86v.

367. The Passion Master: *Adoration of the Magi*. Paris, Bibl. nat., lat. 1052, fol. 39v.

368 and 369. The Passion Master: *Annunciation*. St. Theobald. Paris, Bibl. nat., lat. 1052, fols. 352 and 416.

370 and 371. The Passion Master: *Massacre of the Innocents. Resurrection*. Paris, Bibl. nat., lat. 1052, fols. 308 and 115v.

372. Follower of Pucelle: *Crucifixion*. Oxford, Bodl. Lib., Douce 313, fol. 234.

373. Follower of Pucelle: *Flagellation*. Oxford, Bodl. Lib., Douce 313, fol. 233v.

374. Pucelle Workshop: *Baptism of Christ.*
Paris, Bibl. nat., lat. 10483, fol. 259.

375. Bondol Workshop (?), *ca.* 1357: *Baptism of Christ.*
London, Brit. Mus., Royal 17 E VII, Vol. II, fol. 134v.

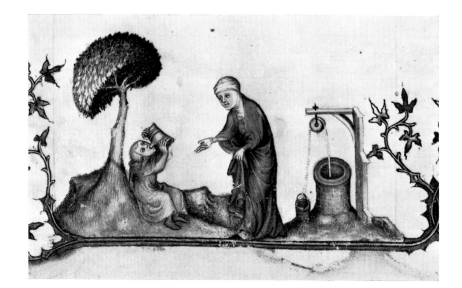

376 and 377. Bondol (?): *Hagar and Ishmael. Abraham and Abimelech.* Paris, Bibl. nat., fr. 15397, fols. 34 and 34v.

378. Bondol Workshop: *Baptism of Christ*.
The Hague, Museum Meermanno-Westreenianum,
ms. 10 B 23, fol. 468.

379. Follower of Bondol: *Baptism of Christ*.
Cambridge, Fitzwilliam Museum,
ms. 3–1954, fol. 62v.

380 and 381. Bondol and Nicolas de Bataille: *Revelation, XIII, 18. Revelation, XII, 13–14*. Angers, Musée des Tapisseries.

382. Bondol: *Jean de Vaudetar Presenting Bible to Charles V*. The Hague, Museum Meermanno-Westreenianum, ms. 10 B 23, fol. 2.
383. Associate of Bondol (?), *ca.* 1357: *Christ and the Evangelists*. London, Brit. Mus., Royal 17 E VII, Vol. I, fol. 1.

384. Associate of Bondol (?), *ca.* 1357: *Parables of Solomon*. London, Brit. Mus., Royal 17 E VII, Vol. II, fol. 1.

385. Associate of Bondol: *Nature Brings "Sens," Rhetoric, Music to the Poet*. Paris, Bibl. nat., fr. 1584, fol. E.

386. Bondol Workshop: *Infancy Scenes*. The Hague, Museum Meermanno-Westreenianum, ms. 10 B 23, fol. 467.

387. Bondol and Bataille Workshop: *Revelation, I, 3*.
Angers, Musée des Tapisseries.

388. Master of the Bellpuig Coronation: *An Evangelist*.
Urbino, Annunziata.

389. Master of the Bellpuig Coronation: *Three Saints* (detail). Bellpuig (destroyed).

390. Ferrer Bassa, *ca.* 1345: *Coronation of the Virgin* (detail).
Barcelona, Pedralbes.

391. Master of the Bellpuig Coronation:
Coronation of the Virgin (detail). Urbino, Annunziata.

392. Master of the Bellpuig Coronation: *Coronation of the Virgin* (detail). Bellpuig (destroyed).

393. Master of the Cité des Dames: *Animals Entering the Ark.*
Paris, Bibl. nat., fr. 9, fol. 15.

394. Bartolo di Fredi: *Animals Entering the Ark.*
S. Gimignano, Collegiata.

395. Roman: *Legend of St. Stephen.*
Béziers, St. Nazaire.

396. Sienese, 1319: *Christ on the Cross.* Tübingen,
Universitätsbibliothek, Phillipps 1398, fol. 91v.

397. Simone Martini: *Madonna of Humility* (sinopia). Avignon, Notre-Dame des Doms.

398 and 399: Cavallinesque, *ca.* 1307: *Angels.* Béziers, St. Nazaire.

400. Master of St. George Codex: *St. George and the Dragon*. Rome, Bibl. Vaticana, Arch. S. Pietro, C129, fol. 85.

401. 17th-century drawing after Simone Martini: *St. George and the Dragon*. Avignon, Notre-Dame des Doms. Rome, Bibl. Vaticana, Barb. lat. 4426, fol. 36.

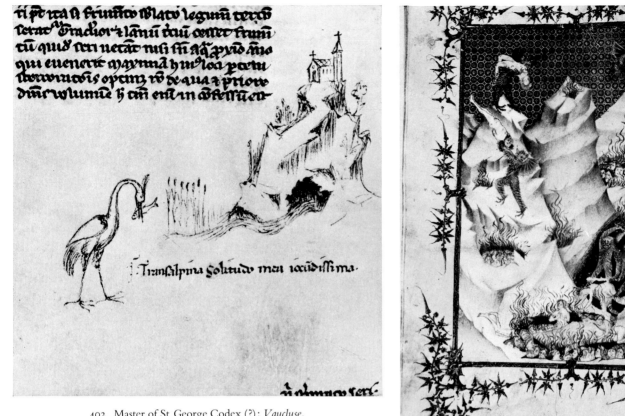

402. Master of St. George Codex (?): *Vaucluse*.
Paris, Bibl. nat., lat. 6802, fol. 143 v.

403. Lombard, 1386: *Inferno*. Rome, Coll. Marchesa Guidi di Bagno.

404. Florentine: *Deposition*. Avignon, St. Didier.

405. Matteo Giovanetti: Figures in the embrasure of the east window. Avignon, Papal Palace, Chapel of St. John.

405a. French, 1405: *Apostles* (detail of *Last Judgment*). Ennezat, near Riom.

406. Matteo Giovanetti, 1353: *Moses*. Avignon, Papal Palace, Salle de l'Audience.
407. Neapolitan: *St. Louis of Toulouse*. Aix, Musée Granet.

409. Neapolitan: *Crucifixion.* Avignon, Musée Calvet, ms. 138, fol. 150v.

408. Neapolitan: *Adam and Eve.* Paris, Bibl. nat., fr. 9561, fol. 8v.

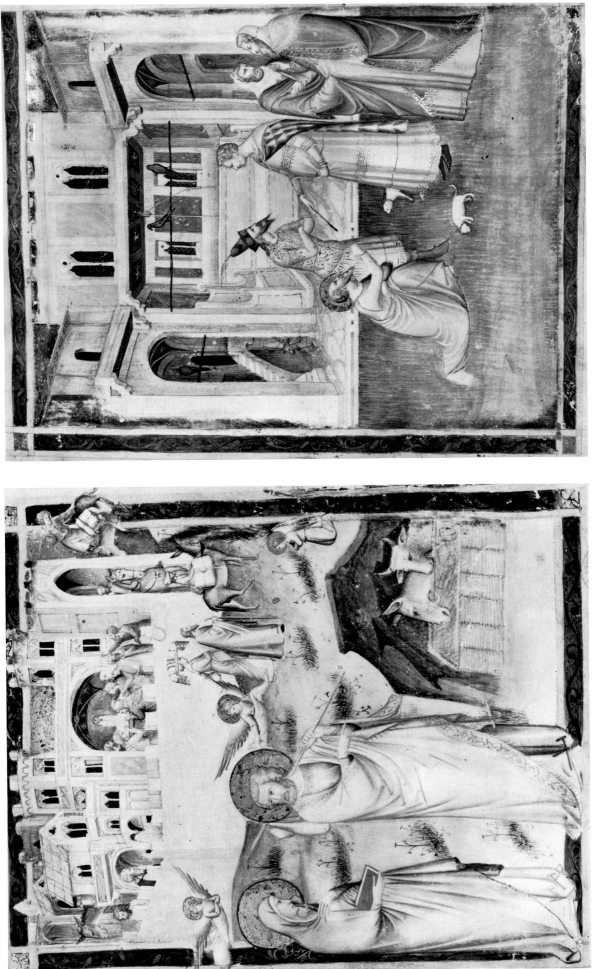

410 and 411. Master of the Angevin Bible: *The Arrival in Bethlehem. Joseph of Arimathea before Pilate.* Paris, Bibl. nat., fr. 9561, fols. 132v and 179.

412. Master of the Angevin Bible: *Angel Appearing to Joseph.*
Paris, Bibl. nat., fr. 9561, fol. 139v.

413. Neapolitan: *Nativity.*
Naples, S. Lorenzo Maggiore, Barresi Chapel.

414. Associate of Master of the Angevin Bible:
Nativity. Aix, Musée Granet.

415. Neapolitan: *Nativity.*
Vienna, Nationalbibliothek, ms. 1921, fol. 228.

416. Neapolitan: *Fool*. Vienna, Nationalbibliothek, ms. 1921, fol. 65v.

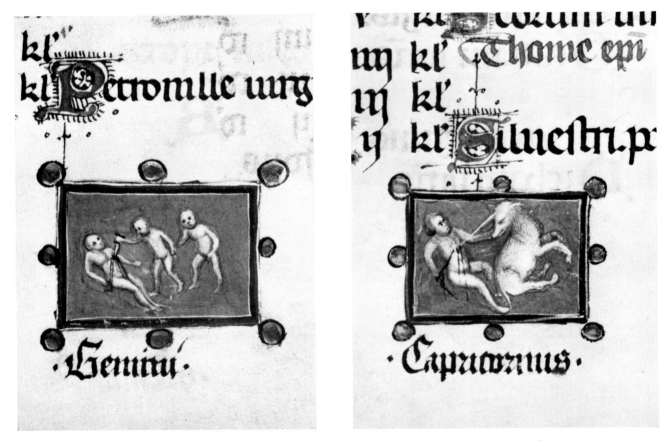

417 and 418. Neapolitan: *Twins. Capricorn*. Vienna, Nationalbibliothek, ms. 1921, fols. 5v and 12v.

419. The Limbourgs: *Château de Lusignan*, detail of *March*. Chantilly, Musée Condé, *Très Riches Heures*, fol. 3v.

420. The Limbourgs: *Château de Dourdan*, detail of *April*. Chantilly, Musée Condé, *Très Riches Heures*, fol. 4v.

421. The Limbourgs: *Château de Poitiers* (?), detail of *July*. Chantilly, Musée Condé, *Très Riches Heures*, fol. 7v.

422. The Limbourgs: *Château d'Étampes*, detail of *August*. Chantilly, Musée Condé, *Très Riches Heures*, fol. 8v.

423. The Limbourgs: *Château de Bicêtre* (?), detail of *September*. Chantilly, Musée Condé, *Très Riches Heures*, fol. 9v.

424. The Limbourgs: Detail from *The Temptation of Christ*, with the Château de Mehun. Chantilly, Musée Condé, *Très Riches Heures*, fol. 161v.

425. Engraving of a drawing of 1737 by Penot of the Château de Mehun.

427. Workshop of the Embriachi: Retable from the Abbey of Poissy. Paris, Louvre.

426. Riom, Ste-Chapelle (interior).

429. Poitiers, Palais: *Cheminée*.

428. Boucicaut Master: *Ostentation of the Relics of the Ste-Chapelle, Paris*. Châteauroux, Bibl. municipale, ms. 2, fol. 350.

430. French, 1465: Detail of *Annunciation* showing the Château de Mehun. New York, The Cloisters.

431. Drawing by Hazé, 1840: Ste-Chapelle, "Galerie du Cerf," and the Palais, Bourges.

432. Drawing, 17th century: Palais and the Ste-Chapelle, Bourges. Paris, Bibl. nat., Cabinet des Estampes.

433. French, early 15th century: *Man of Sorrows*. Bourges, Musée Jacques Cœur.

434 and 435. Poitiers, Palais. Capitals of the *Cheminée*.

436. French, towards 1400: *Queen Isabeau de Bavière* (after cast).
Poitiers, Palais, *Cheminée*.

437. French, towards 1400: *Duchess Jeanne de Boulogne* (after cast).
Poitiers, Palais, *Cheminée*.

438. Workshop of Master of the Coronation: *The Land of the Tartars*. Paris, Bibl. nat., fr. 12201, fol. 17v.

439. Adelphoe Master: *Livre de la chasse (Prologue)*. Paris, Bibl. nat., fr. 616, fol. 13.

440. French, before 1408: Frontispiece to *Comédies* of Terence. Paris, Bibl. nat., lat. 7907A, fol. 2v.

441. Byzantine: *Manuel II Paleologus*.
Paris, Bibl. nat., Suppl. gr. 309, fol. VI.

442. The Limbourgs: *Adoration of the Cross* (detail).
Chantilly, Musée Condé, *Très Riches Heures*, fol. 193.

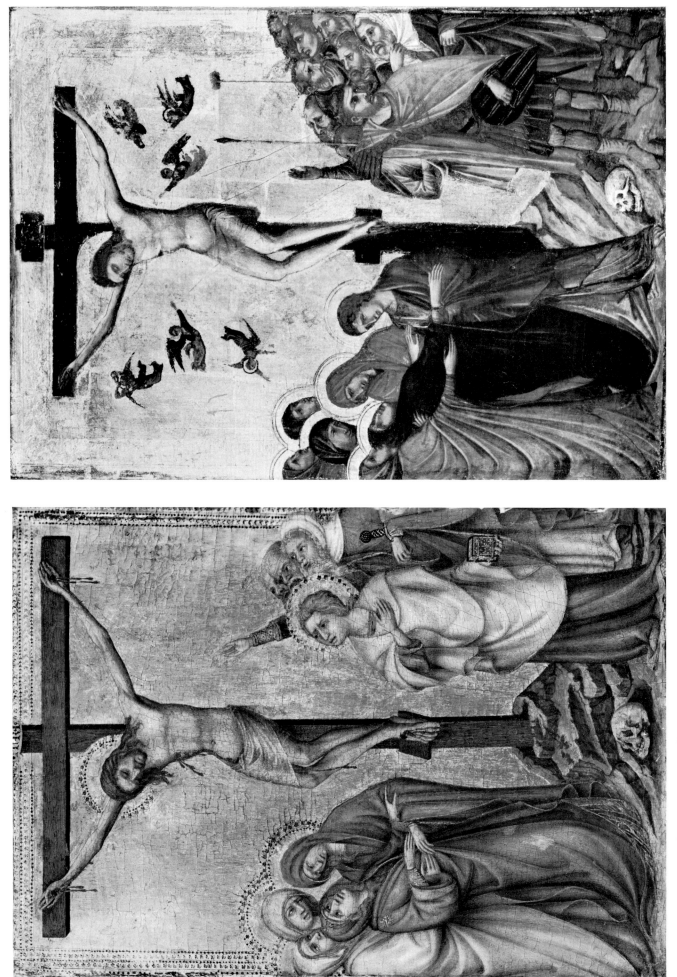

443. French (?), *ca.* 1380: *Crucifixion.* Brussels, Musées Royaux.

444. Ducciesque: *Crucifixion.* New York, Historical Society.

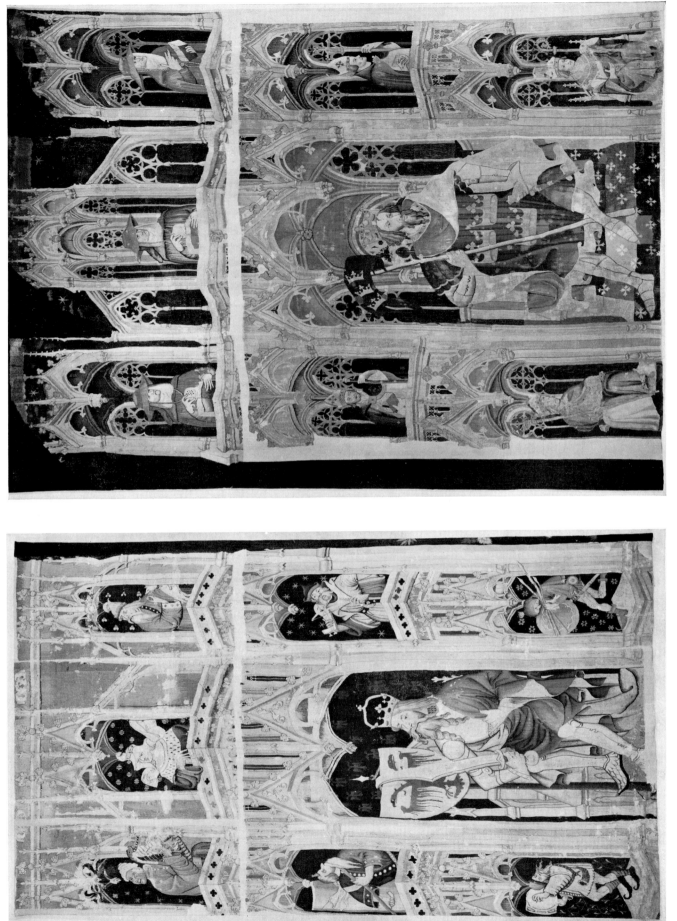

445 and 446. French, late 14th century: *Julius Caesar with Courtiers. King Arthur with Ecclesiastics*, from the Berry tapestries. New York, The Cloisters.

447. Florentine embroidery: *The Nativity* (detail).
Whereabouts unknown.

448. "Ugolino Lorenzetti" (Bartolommeo Bulgarini):
Nativity. Cambridge (Mass.), Fogg Art Museum.

449. Geri di Lapo: *Crucifixion*, detail of embroidered altar hanging. Manresa, Cathedral.

450 and 451: Drawing by Montfaucon of part of the embroidered retable given by Jean de Berry to the Cathedral of Chartres:
St. John the Baptist, Charlemagne, and Louis of Toulouse with Charles V and two sons;
Sts. Catherine and Louis with Queen Jeanne de Bourbon and two daughters.

452. Florentine embroidery: *Adoration of the Magi*. New York, Coll. R. Lehman.

454. Flemish, before 1401: *Annunciation*, *Visitation*. Lucca, Opera del Duomo.

453. 12th-century *Madonna*
from S. Gangolf, Metz. Bryn Athyn,
Coll. Raymond Pitcairn.

455. Flemish, before 1401: *Crucifixion*. Lucca, Opera del Duomo.

456. Roman: *Agrippina Maior as Juno*,
from the Ste-Chapelle, Bourges. Paris, Louvre.

457. Italian (?), 13th century: *Ruler and angels*,
from the Ste-Chapelle, Bourges. Paris, Louvre.

458. Roman: *Jupiter*,
from the Ste-Chapelle, Bourges. Paris, Louvre.

459. Roman: *Jupiter*,
from the Ste-Chapelle, Bourges. Paris, Louvre.

460. Renaissance (Venetian?): Cameo from Bourges. Paris, Louvre.

461. Roman: *Agrippina Maior as Juno*, from the Ste-Chapelle, Bourges. Paris, Louvre.

462 and 463: French (?), before 1402: *Constantine. Allegory of Salvation*. Paris, Bibl. nat., Cabinet des Médailles.

464 and 465. French (?), before 1402: *Heraclius. Heraclius with the Cross*. Paris, Bibl. nat., Cabinet des Médailles.

466. French: *Madonna*. Berlin-Dahlem, Staatl. Museen.

467. Roman, 4th century: *Venus at her Toilet*. Paris, Petit Palais.

468. Shortly before 1390:
Medal of Francesco Carrara.

469. Seal of Renaud de Montfaucon, 1218.
Paris, Arch. nat., J394, no. 56.

470. Byzantine: *Annunciation to Anna*.
Rome, Bibl. Vaticana,
Vat. gr. 1162, fol. 16.

471. French, *ca.* 1390: *Royal Cup* (cover with the Legend of St. Agnes). London, Brit. Mus.

472. Yellow agate cup, from the Ste-Chapelle, Bourges. Bourges, Musée Jacques Cœur.

473. French, *ca.* 1390: *Royal Cup*. London, Brit. Mus.

474. Great Seal of Jean de Berry, 1370 or earlier.
Paris, Arch. nat., J185 (B), no. 45.

475. Initial K (Charles V giving a piece of the Cross to
Jean de Berry), 1372. Paris, Arch. nat., AE II 393.

476. Marriage Contract of the Duke and Jeanne de Boulogne, 1389.
Paris, Arch. nat., AE II 411.

477. Seal of Jean de Berry, 1397.
Bourges, Arch. du Cher, *liasse* 140, T306.

478. French painter, *ca.* 1390: *Jean de Berry kneeling between SS. Andrew and John the Baptist.* – 479. Jacquemart: *Jean de Berry with SS. Andrew and John the Baptist before the Virgin.* Brussels, Bibl. Royale, ms. 11060–1, pp. 10 and 14. (details of Figs. 179 and 181).

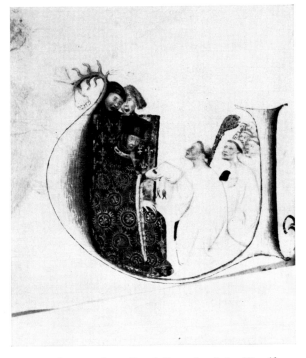

480. Bruges painter: *Jean de Berry Associating Himself with St. Barthélemy de Bruges.* Paris, Arch. nat., AE II 422.

481. Copy of the Limbourgs, 1405: *Jean de Berry Investing the Canons of the Ste-Chapelle, Bourges* (after Bastard).

482. Seal of the Treasurer of the Ste-Chapelle, Bourges, 1405. Paris, Bibl. nat., Cabinet des Médailles.

483. Luçon Master, *ca.* 1406: *Procession with Jean de Berry* (?). Paris, Bibl. nat., lat. 8886, fol. 318v.

484. Pseudo-Jacquemart: *Joachim's offering rejected; Duke of Berry adoring Virgin and Child.* Paris, Bibl. nat., lat. 919, fol. 8 (detail of Fig. 219).

485. Bedford Master and associate: *Jean de Berry and Companions before St. Peter*. Paris, Bibl. nat., lat. 919, fol. 96 (detail of Fig. 231).

786. Luçon Workshop, 1410: *Jacques Legrand Presents Book to Berry*. Paris, Bibl. nat., fr. 1023, fol. 2.

487. Boucicaut Workshop, 1409: *Salmon Presents His Manuscript to Charles VI* (detail). Paris, Bibl. nat., fr. 23279, fol. 53.

488. Baptist Master: *Jean de Berry before the Madonna* (detail). *Heures de Turin*, fol. 78v (burned).

489. The Limbourgs: *January*. Chantilly, Musée Condé, *Très Riches Heures*, fol. 1 v.

490. Copy after the Limbourgs: *Jean de Berry*. Paris, Bibl. nat.,
Cabinet des Estampes, Gaignières Oa 13 Rés., fol. 15.

491. Parement Master (retouched), *ca.* 1385: *Jean de Berry*.
Turin, Museo Civico, "*Heures de Milan*," fol. 87.

492. Parement Workshop: *Jean de Berry (?) before Christ, the Virgin and St. John.*
Paris, Louvre, Cabinet des Dessins (from the *Très Belles Heures de Notre-Dame*).

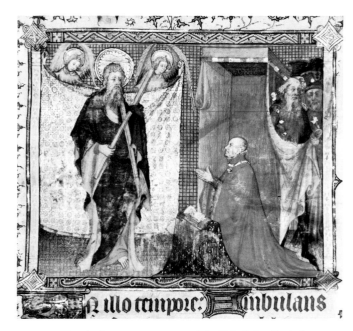

493. Pseudo-Jacquemart, *ca.* 1410: *The Duke before St. Andrew.* Bourges, Bibl. municipale, ms. 48, fol. 181.

494. Embriachi Workshop: *The Duke, His Patron Saints, and an Angel* (detail of altarpiece from Poissy). Paris, Louvre.

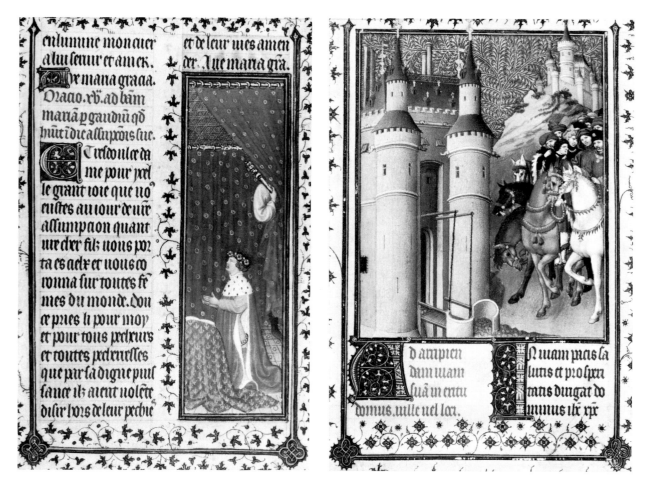

495. The Limbourgs, *ca.* 1410: *The Duke at Prayer.* – 496. The Limbourgs, *ca.* 1409–10: *The Duke and His Party Arriving at a Château.* New York, The Cloisters, *Belles Heures*, fols. 91 and 223v.

497. Copy of the Limbourgs: Lost illustration of the Itinerary from the *Très Belles Heures de Notre-Dame* (after Bastard).

498. The Limbourgs: *The Duke Beginning a Journey*. Paris, Bibl. nat., lat. 18014, fol. 288v.

499. Boucicaut Workshop, *ca.* 1410: *The Duke before St. Andrew*. Bourges, Bibl. municipale, ms. 35, fol. 17v.

500. Cité des Dames Workshop: *Premierfait Giving Manuscript of Boccaccio to the Duke*. Paris, Bibl. nat., fr. 131, fol. 1.

502. Jean de Cambrai: Effigy of Jean de Berry (detail). Bourges, Cathedral.

501. Jean de Cambrai: Head of Jean de Berry. Bourges, Musée Jacques Cœur.

504. Boucicaut Workshop: *Precious Stones Offered to Jean de Berry* (?). Paris, Bibl. nat., fr. 9141, fol. 235v.

503. French illuminator: *Premierfait Giving Manuscript of Boccaccio to the Duke.* Paris, Bibl. nat., fr. 226, fol. 1.

505. French: Portrait of Louis II d'Anjou. Paris, Bibl. nat., Cabinet des Estampes (Borders modern).

506. Early copy of a contemporary portrait of Jean sans Peur. Paris, Louvre.

LOVIS·DDANOV·R·DE·NAPLE·SICILE·&·

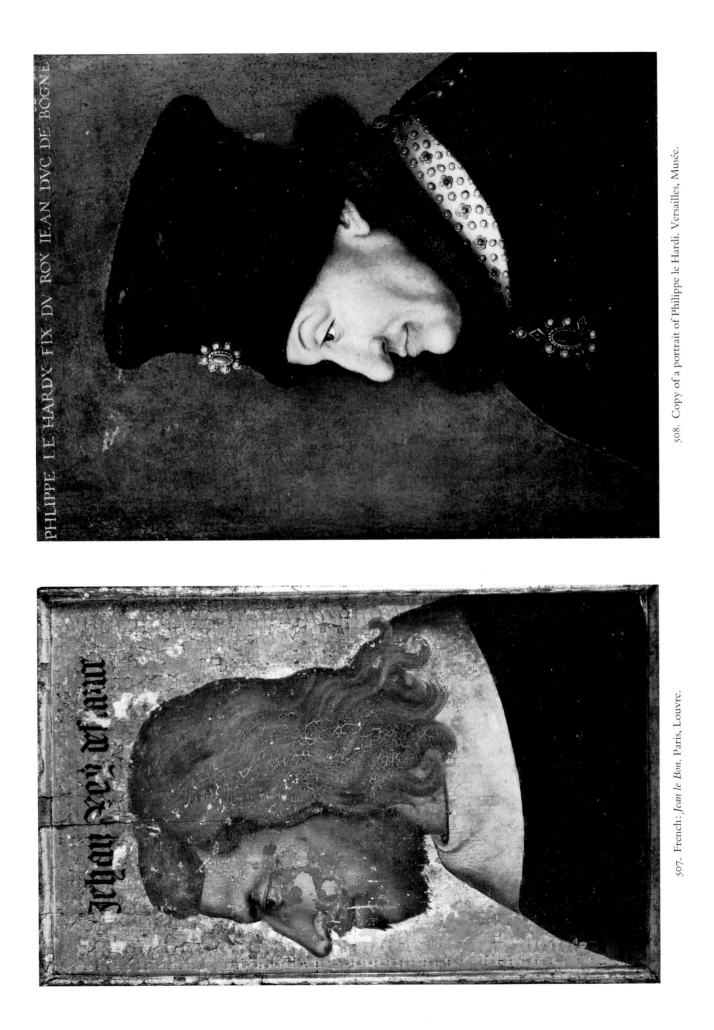

507. French: *Jean le Bon*. Paris, Louvre.

508. Copy of a portrait of Philippe le Hardi. Versailles, Musée.

509. French, early and later 15th century: *Reliquary of Ste. Valérie*. Chambon-sur-Voueize, Church.

510 and 511. Hans Holbein the Younger: *Jeanne de Boulogne*; *Jean de Berry* (after statues in Ste-Chapelle, Bourges).
Basel, Öffentliche Kunstsammlung.

512. French, before 1419: Ring with portrait of Jean sans Peur.
Paris, Coll. Comte Blaise de Montesquiou.

513. Maso di Banco: *Christ Judging*.
Florence, S. Croce, Chapel of S. Silvestro.

514. Follower of Altichiero: *St. James Led from the City*.
Padua, Santo, Chapel of S. Felice.

515. St. Peter Master: *Peter Receiving Souls*
(detail of *Last Judgment*). Grosseto, Museo Diocesano.

516. French, *ca.* 1415: *Peter Receiving Souls.*
Private Collection.

517. Follower of Bondol: *A French King at a Lecture.*
Brussels, Bibl. Royale, ms. 9505–6, fol. 2v.

518. The Limbourgs, *ca.* 1410: *Jeanne de Boulogne.*
New York, The Cloisters, *Belles Heures*, fol. 91v.

519. Bondol Workshop: *Crucifixion*. Cleveland, Museum of Art, *Gotha Missal*, fol. 63v.

520. Arms of Jean de Berry (*France moderne*).
Poitiers, Palais, *Cheminée*.

521. Figure holding shield of Jeanne de Boulogne (after 1389).
Poitiers, Palais, *Cheminée*.

523. Secret seal of Jean de Berry, 1372.
Paris, Arch. nat., J211, no. 41.

522. Counter-seal of Jean de Berry, 1397 and 1410. Bourges, Arch. du Cher, *liasse* 140 (T. Sc. 306).

524. French, *ca.* 1370: *St. Louis as Charles V.* Paris, Louvre.

525. French, *ca.* 1340: Mitre, *Annunciation*. Sixt, Abbey Church.

526. French: Mitre, *Entombment*. Paris, Musée de Cluny.

527. Follower of Ambrogio Lorenzetti:
Crucifixion (detail). Rome, Pinacoteca Vaticana.

528. Master of Città di Castello: *Crucifixion* (detail).
Balcarres (Fife), Earl of Crawford.

529. Roman painter, *ca.* 1300: *Crucifixion*. Stimigliano, S. Maria in Vescovio.

530. Giottesque: *Crucifixion* (detail). Whereabouts unknown.

531. Roman: *Tropaeum and Captives*. Mainz, Römisch-Germanisches Museum.

570. *St. Joseph* (detail of Fig. 8).

536. Follower of Pucelle: *Crucifixion*. Oxford, Bodl. Lib., Douce 313, fol. 4.

538. Barna: *Way to Calvary*. S. Gimignano, Collegiata.

537. Copy of Jan van Eyck: *Crucifixion*. Turin, Museo Civico, *Heures de Milan*, fol. 48v.

540. Simone Martini: *Obsequies of St. Martin.* Assisi, S. Francesco.

539. Jacopo di Cione: *Coronation of the Virgin.* Florence, Accademia.

541. Workshop of Pucelle: *Christ and the Apostles*.
Chantilly, Musée Condé, ms. 51, fol. 124v.

542. French, *ca.* 1235: *Death of the Virgin* (detail).
Strasbourg, Cathedral.

543. Byzantine, 13th century: *Agony in the Garden*.
Berlin, Staatsbibliothek, gr. qu. 66, fol. 87v.

544. Pucelle Workshop: *Crucifixion*.
Heures de Jeanne de Navarre, fol. 112. Whereabouts unknown.

545. French, *ca.* 1375: *Man of Sorrows and Wound.*
New York, Morgan Library, ms. 90, fol. 130.

546. Vitale da Bologna: *Man of Sorrows.*
Florence, Coll. R. Longhi.

547. Circle of Altichiero: *Man of Sorrows* (damaged). Padua, Santo, Chapel of S. Felice.

548. Metz, early 14th century: *Madonna*. Birmingham, Barber Institute, *Horae*, fol. 14v. – 549. Metz, third quarter of the 14th century: *Madonna of Humility*. Whereabouts unknown. – 550. Metz, third quarter of the 14th century: *Madonna of Humility*. New York, Morgan Library, ms. 88, fol. 151.

551. Bohemian: *Adoration of the Magi*, Prague, Library of the Cathedral, Cim. VI, fol. 32.
552. Bohemian, 1370–75: *Madonna with Emperor Charles IV, His Son, and Saints*. Prague, Národní Galerie.

553. Domenico di Niccolo: *Nativity*.
Siena, Palazzo Pubblico, Cappella del Popolo.

554. Masaccio, 1422: *Madonna*.
Cascia, S. Giovenale.

555. Masaccio, *ca.* 1424: *Christ Child* (detail). Florence, Uffizi.

556. Etruscan: Votive figure. Rome, Musei Vaticani.

557. Austrian, 1370–72: *Nativity*.
Meran, Schloss Tirol.

558. Lombard, *ca.* 1385: *Birth of the Virgin*.
Paris, Bibl. nat., lat. 757, fol. 351v.

559. Master of S. Mark (Arnau Bassa): *Crucifixion*.
New York, Morgan Library.

560. Lombard, *ca.* 1385: *Madonna and Donor*.
Paris, Bibl. nat., lat. 757, fol. 109v.

561. Master of Berry's Cleres Femmes, 1402–3: *Caritas Romana.*
Paris, Bibl. nat., fr. 598, fol. 99.

562. Pucelle and collaborator: *Miracle of the Virgin.*
Paris, Bibl. nat., nouv. acq. fr. 24541, fol. 39v.

563. North French, *ca.* 1325: *Vigils of the Dead.*
Baltimore, Walters Art Gallery, ms. 90, fol. 194v.

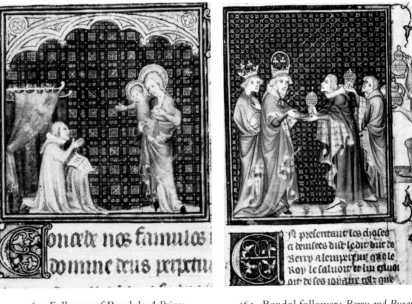

564. Follower of Bondol: *A Prince
before the Virgin and Child.* Cambridge,
Fitzwilliam Museum, ms. 3–1954, fol. 451.

565. Bondol follower: *Berry and Burgundy
Giving Gifts to Emperor Charles IV.*
Paris, Bibl. nat., fr. 2813, fol. 478v.

567. Bohemian, before 1364: *Presentation in the Temple*. Prague, Národní Muzeum, ms. XVI.D.13.

566. Bohemian, before 1364: *Annunciation*. Prague, Národní Muzeum, ms. XVI.D.13.

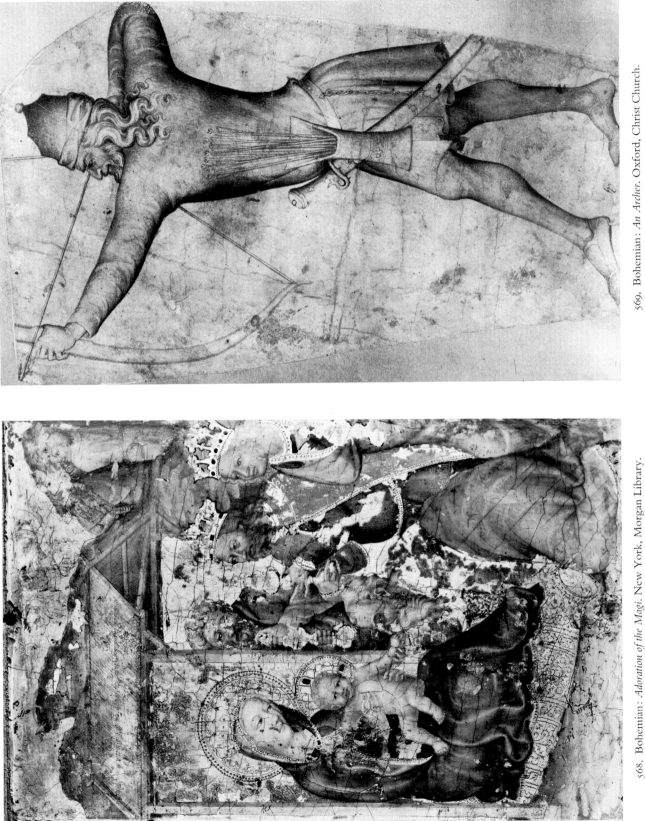

569. Bohemian: *An Archer*. Oxford, Christ Church.

568. Bohemian: *Adoration of the Magi*. New York, Morgan Library.

570. *St. Joseph* (detail of Fig. 8).

571. French, *ca.* 1400: Jean de Berry's *Reliquary of the Thorn*. London, British Museum.

572. French, *ca.* 1405: Triptych. Amsterdam, Rijksmuseum.

573. French, before 1404: *Goldenes Rössl* (detail).
Altötting, Pilgrimage Church.

574. French, *ca.* 1400: Reliquary
of the *Ordre du St-Esprit* (detail). Paris, Louvre.

575. Early 14th century: *Pala d'Oro* (detail). Venice, S. Marco.

576. Copy of a *joyau* of Charles VI and Isabeau de Bavière.
Munich, Bayr. Nationalmuseum.

577. French, *ca.* 1415: *St. John the Baptist*.
Florence, Museo Nazionale.

578. Giovannino dei Grassi: *The Lord over the Water*. Florence, Bibl. Nazionale, Landau–Finaly 22, fol. 26.

579. Giovannino dei Grassi: *The Lord Dividing the Land from the Water*. Florence, Bibl. Nazionale, Landau-Finaly 22, fol. 30.

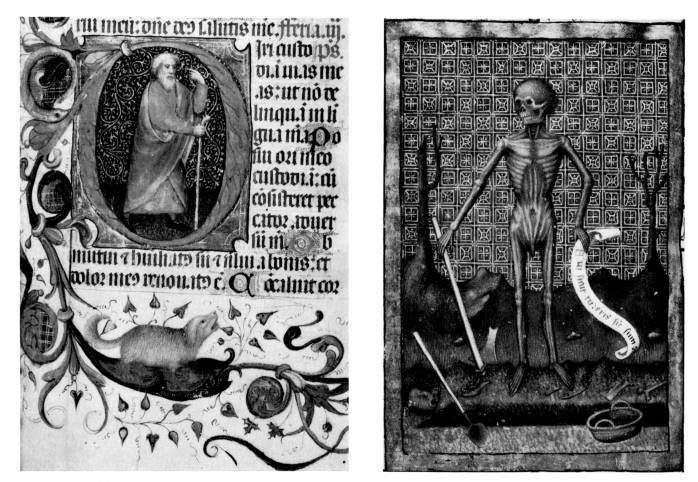

580 and 581. Spanish follower of Giovannino: Illustration of Psalm. *Missa pro Defunctis*. Barcelona, Archivo Histórico, *Horae*, fol. 32 and unnumbered folio.

582. Michelino, *ca.* 1414: *Nativity*.
London, Brit. Mus., Egerton 3266, fol. 15.

583. French, *ca.* 1380: *Abraham and Sarah*.
Paris, Bibl. nat., fr. 15397, fol. 27v.

584. Lombard, *ca.* 1385: *Missa pro Defunctis.* Paris, Bibl. nat., lat. 757, fol. 237v.

585. Lombard, *ca.* 1380: Scene in *Giron le Courtois.* Paris, Bibl. nat., nouv. acq. fr. 5243, fol. 34.

586. Catalan, *ca.* 1393: *St. Luke*. Vich, Diocesan Museum.

587. Copy *ca.* 1400 of Beauneveu (?): *Death, Assumption and Coronation of the Virgin.*
Paris, Louvre, Cabinet des Dessins.

588. Nuremberg (?), *ca.* 1365: *Death and Coronation of St. Clare.* Nuremberg, Germanisches Nationalmuseum.

589 and 590. Beauneveu and assistants: *Jean le Bon* (detail). *Philippe VI* (detail). St. Denis, Cathedral.

591. André Beauneveu: *Charles V* (detail). St. Denis, Cathedral.

592. Workshop of Parler: *Rector Radecz*. Prague, Cathedral, Triforium.

593. Workshop of Beauneveu: *A Prophet* (detail).
Bourges, Musée Jacques Cœur.

594. Beauneveu: *A Prophet* (detail).
Bourges, Musée Jacques Cœur.

595. Workshop of Beauneveu: *A Prophet* (detail).
Bourges, Musée Jacques Cœur.

596. French: A head from Mehun-sur-Yèvre.
Paris, Louvre.

597. Beauneveu and associates: Apostles from the Ste-Chapelle. Bourges, Cathedral.

598 and 599. Beauneveu and associates: Apostles (details). Bourges, Cathedral.

600. Workshop of Pucelle: *Trinity*. Chantilly, Musée Condé, ms. 51, fol. 73. – 601. Associate of Pucelle: *Trinity*. *Heures de Jeanne de Navarre*, fol. 129. Whereabouts unknown. – 602. French, 1380–85: *Trinity*. Paris, Bibl. nat., fr. 20090, fol. 281v.

603. Follower of Bondol, 1368: *Trinity*. Berlin, Staatsbibliothek, Phillipps 1906, fol. 8.

604–606. Workshop of Pucelle: *Salvum me fac. The Fool. Three Clerics Singing.* Chantilly, Musée Condé, ms. 51, fols. 43v, 35v, 63.

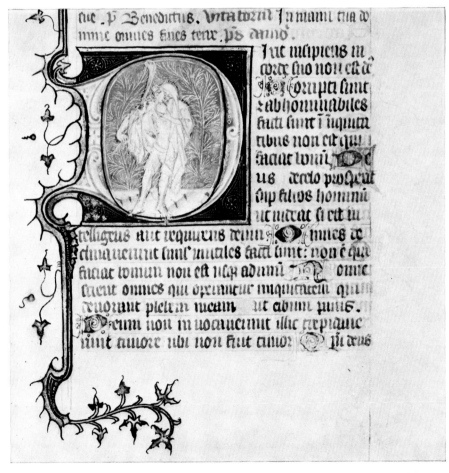

607. Workshop of Pseudo-Jacquemart: *The Fool.* Bourges, Bibl. municipale, ms. 16, fol. 36.

In omnem terram exiuit   vlla puuerencie en la cog

608 and 609. French, *ca.* 1375: *St. Louis of Toulouse. A Prince before St. Andrew*. Cambridge, Fitzwilliam Museum, ms. 3–1954, fols. 496, 464.
610. Workshop of Pseudo-Jacquemart, 1382: *St. Andrew*. London, Brit. Mus., Royal 19 B XVII, fol. 9v.

Es paraboles salmo   lage pur oyr. Et celuy qui entent bien en la

611. French, 1380–85: *Story of Solomon*. Paris, Bibl. nat., fr. 20090, fol. 290.

612. Pseudo-Jacquemart, 1382: *St. Jerome*. London, Brit. Mus., Royal 19 B XVII, fol. 2. – 613. Pucelle: *Funeral Service*. Paris, Musée Jacquemart-André, *Heures de Jeanne de Savoie*, fol. 116. – 614. Lombard, *ca.* 1390: *Nailing Christ to the Cross*. Parma, Bibl. Palatina, ms. 56, fol. 137v.

615. Pseudo-Jacquemart, 1382: *Coronation, Saints, Last Judgment*. London, Brit. Mus., Royal 19 B XVII, fol. 5.

616. Follower of Jacquemart, *ca.* 1390: *Nativity*.
Baltimore, Walters Art Gallery, ms. 96, fol. 60.

617. Follower of Jacquemart: *Nativity*.
London, Brit. Mus., Harley 4382, fol. 159.

618. Follower of Jacquemart, *ca.* 1390: *Annunciation*.
Baltimore, Walters Art Gallery, ms. 96, fol. 30.

619. Ghent (?), 1366: *Nativity*. The Hague,
Museum Meermanno-Westreenianum, ms. 10.A.14, fol. 22.

620. French, *ca.* 1395: *Annunciation.*
London, Brit. Mus., Add. 23145, fol. 44.

621. Follower of Jacquemart, *ca.* 1390: *Vigils of the Dead.*
Baltimore, Walters Art Gallery, ms. 96, fol. 138.

622. Follower of Jacquemart: *Man of Sorrows.*
London, Brit. Mus., Harley 4382, fol. 182v.

623. English, *ca.* 1300: *Crucifixion.*
Baltimore, Walters Art Gallery, ms. 102, fol. 77v.

624. Follower of Jacquemart: *Jealous Man Beating his Wife*.
Paris, Bibl. nat., fr. 380, fol. 62v.

625. Metz, *ca.* 1385: *Madonna*.
Paris, Bibl. nat., lat. 1403, fol. 15.

626 and 627. Circle of Pseudo-Jacquemart: *Adoration of the Magi. Trinity*. Baltimore, Walters Art Gallery, ms. 94, fols. 60v and 84.

628. Ambrogio Lorenzetti: *Annunciation*. Siena, Pinacoteca.

629. Guelders (?), early 15th century: *Nativity*.
Antwerp, Musée Mayer van den Bergh.

630. Giovannino dei Grassi: *Nativity*.
Florence, Bibl. Naz., Landau-Finaly 22, fol. 11.

631 and 632. Workshop of Barna: *Madonna* and *Man of Sorrows*. Florence, Horne Museum.

633. French, *ca.* 1400: *Madonna*.
New York, The Frick Collection.

634. Bartolommeo da Camogli, 1346: *Madonna of Humility*.
Palermo, Museo Nazionale.

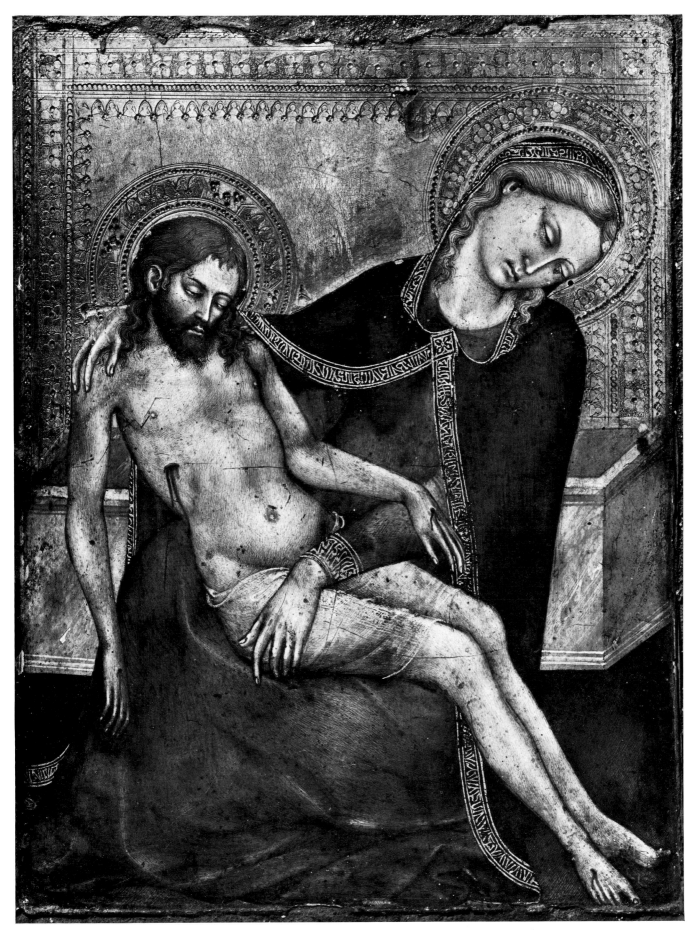

635. Giovanni da Milano: *Vesperbild*. Paris, Coll. Comtesse L. du Luart.

636. Roger van der Weyden: *Lamentation*.
Berlin-Dahlem, Staatl. Museen.

637. German, *ca.* 1330: *Vesperbild*.
Bonn, Rheinisches Landesmuseum.

638. Cecco di Pietro, 1377: *Vesperbild*. Pisa, Museo Civico.

639. Tuscan, *ca.* 1365: *Vesperbild*. Volterra, Palazzo dei Priori.

640. Master of the Pietà: *Vesperbild*.
Detroit, Institute of Arts.

641. Master of the Pietà: *Vesperbild*.
Angers, Musée David.

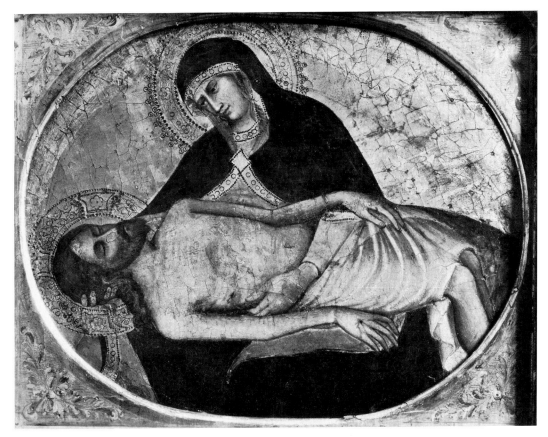

642. Florentine, *ca.* 1400: *Lamentation* (fragment). Rotterdam, Boymans Museum.

644. English, early 14th century: *Virgin with the Dead Christ*.
London, Brit. Mus., Yates Thompson 13, fol. 123v.

643. Luçon Master, 1410: *Death and a Nobleman*. Paris, Bibl. nat., fr. 1023, fol. 74.

645. St. Francis Master: *Lamentation*. Perugia, Pinacoteca.

646. Metz, *ca.* 1385: *Lamentation*.
Paris, Bibl. nat., lat. 1403, fol. 61.

647. Workshop of Taddeo Gaddi, 1336:
Lamentation. Naples, Museo di Capodimonte.

654. Workshop of Jacquema[...]
Presented to Alexander. Oxfor[...]

648. Tournai, *ca.* 1400: *Lamentation*.
Paris, Bibl. nat., lat. 1364, fol. 105v.

650. French, *ca.* 1405: *Vesperbild*. Baltimore,
Walters Art Gallery, ms. 100, fol. 34.

656 and 657. French, bef[...]

649. Utrecht, early 15th century: *Lamentation*. Baltimore, Walters Art Gallery, ms. 185, fol. 79v.

651. Ta
Fl

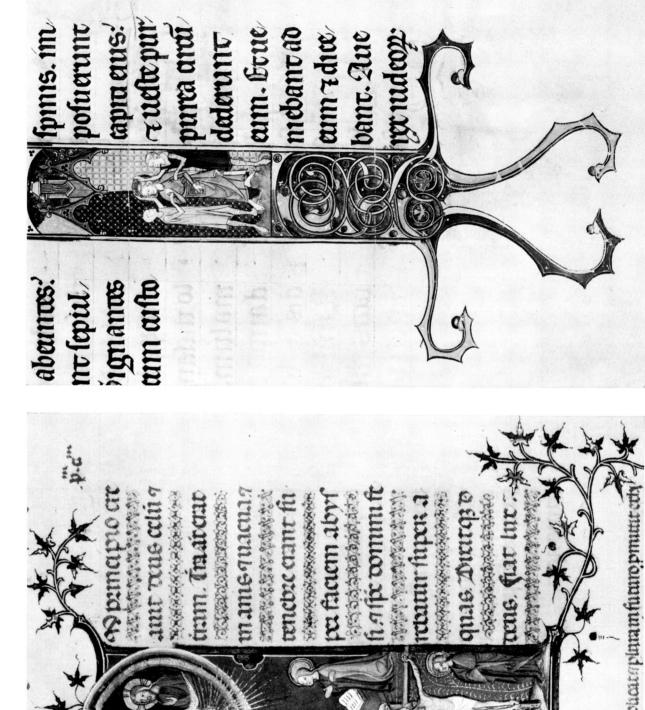

659. French, *ca.* 1280: *Crowning with Thorns.*
Paris, Bibl. nat., lat. 8892, fol. 29.

658. French illuminator, 1388–90: *Trinity, Annunciation and Crucifixion.*
Rome, Bibl. Vaticana, lat. 50, fol. 5v.

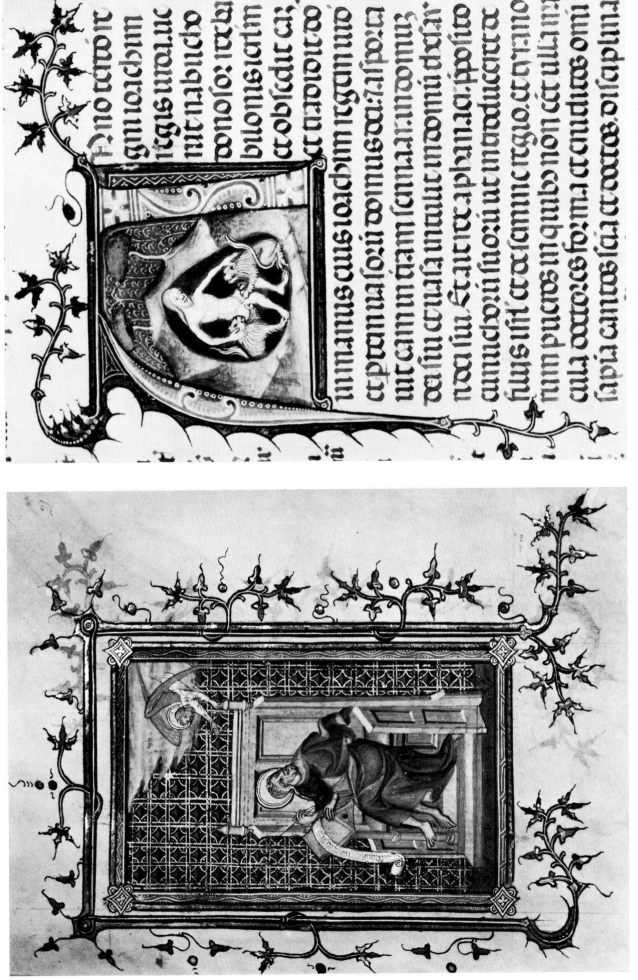

661. French illuminator, 1388–90: *Daniel in the Lions' Den.*
Rome, Bibl. Vaticana, lat. 51, fol. 142v.

660. French, *ca.* 1395: *St. Matthew.*
London, Brit. Mus., Add. 23145, fol. 21.

662. French illuminator, 1388–90: *Madonna of Humility*.
Rome, Bibl. Vaticana, lat. 50, fol. 332v.

663. Follower of Pucelle: *Annunciation*.
Oxford, Bodl. Lib., Douce 313, fol. 5v.

664. French, *ca.* 1400: Brooch with camel.
Florence, Museo Nazionale.

666. *Veronica*. Brussels, Bibl. Royale, ms. 11035–7, fol. 8v.

665. Early 15th century: *Veronica*. Brussels, Bibl. Royale, 11060–61, p. 8.

667. Luçon Workshop, 1406: *Madonna with Marie de Berry and an Attendant*. Paris, Bibl. nat., fr. 926, fol. 2.

668. French, *ca.* 1415: *Madonna on the Moon*.
Brussels, Bibl. Royale, ms. 11035–7, fol. 6v.

669. French, late 14th century:
Madonna with the Writing Child. Paris, Louvre.

670. French, 1412–15: *Simon Alegret and his Nephews presented to the Madonna by St. Simon* (detail). Bourges, Cathedral.

672. Late 14th century: *St. Catherine* (detail). Courtrai, Notre-Dame.

671. Giovanni da Milano: Head of the High Priest (detail of *Expulsion of Joachim*). Florence, S. Croce.

673. Follower of Ambrogio Lorenzetti: *Crucifixion*.
Frankfurt, Städel.

674. Simone Martini: *Crucifixion*.
Antwerp, Musée des Beaux-Arts.

675. Simone Martini: *Way to Calvary*.
Paris, Louvre.

676. Simone Martini: *Deposition*.
Antwerp, Musée des Beaux-Arts.

677. Follower of Pucelle: *Deposition and Bearing of the Body*.
Oxford, Bodl. Lib., Douce 313, fol. 235v.

678. Master of the Bréviaire de Jean sans Peur: *Crucifixion*.
London, Brit. Mus., Add. 35311, fol. 333v.

679. Close to Pietro Lorenzetti: *Allegory of Redemption*. Siena, Pinacoteca.

680. Simone Martini: *A Miracle of Agostino Novello*. Siena, S. Agostino.

681. Roman: *Ulysses and the Sirens.*
London, British Museum.

682. Boucicaut Workshop: *The Divisions of the World.*
Paris, Bibl. nat., fr. 9141, fol. 217v.

683. Follower of Jacquemart: *Story of Joseph.* Paris, Bibl. nat., fr. 247, fol. 25.

684. Ambrogio Lorenzetti: Landscape. Siena, Pinacoteca.

685. Simone Martini, 1328: *Guidoriccio dei Fogliani*. Siena, Palazzo Pubblico.

686 and 687. Ambrogio Lorenzetti: *Ager Senensis* (details). Siena, Palazzo Pubblico.

688. Pietro Lorenzetti: *Deposition*. Assisi, S. Francesco.

689. Pietro Lorenzetti and associates: *Way to Calvary*. Assisi, S. Francesco.

690. Niccolo di Tommaso: *Nativity with St. Bridget*. Rome, Pinacoteca Vaticana.

691. Altichiero: *Adoration of the Shepherds*. Padua, S. Giorgio.

692 and 693. Simone Martini: *Annunciation.* Antwerp, Musée des Beaux-Arts.

695. French, 1390–1400: *Entombment*. Paris, Louvre.

694. French, 1390–1400: *Man of Sorrows*. Troyes, Musée.

696. Altichiero: *Madonna with Giorgio Cavalli* (detail). Verona, S. Anastasia. 697. Pietro Lorenzetti: *Madonna* (detail). Siena, S. Domenico.

698. Ambrogio Lorenzetti: *Madonna* (detail).
Massa Marittima, Museo.

699. Nardo di Cione, 1356 (?): *Madonna* (detail).
New York, Historical Society.

700. Giottesque: *Coronation of the Virgin* (detail). Budapest, Museum of Fine Arts.

701. Riminese: *Adoration of the Magi and Bathing of Christ*.
London, Courtauld Institute.

702. Niccolo di Tommaso: *Coronation of the Virgin*.
Baltimore, Walters Art Gallery.

703. Ambrogio Lorenzetti: *Good Government* (detail).
Siena, Palazzo Pubblico.

704. Deodato Orlandi: *Visitation*.
Berlin-Dahlem, Staatl. Museen.

705. Master of Luçon, 1401: *Coronation of the Virgin*.
Barcelona, Bibl. Central, ms. 1850, fol. 90.

706. Cité des Dames Master, 1401: *Man of Sorrows*.
Barcelona, Bibl. Central, ms. 1850, fol. 1 v.

707. Giovanni da Milano: *Angel Gabriel*.
Prato, Galleria Comunale.

708. Simone Martini, 1333: *Virgin Annunciate* (detail).
Florence, Uffizi.

709. Ugolino di Vieri, 1338: *Annunciation* (detail).
Orvieto, Cathedral.

710. Ferrer Bassa: *Annunciation* (detail).
Pedralbes, Monastery.

711. Broederlam, 1394-99: *Annunciation and Visitation.* Dijon, Musée des Beaux-Arts.

712. Ambrogio Lorenzetti, 1342: *Presentation in the Temple.* Florence, Uffizi.

713. Altichiero and assistants: *St. James Preaching*. Padua, Santo.

714 and 715. Brussels Initials Master: *February*. *March*. Parma, Bibl. Palatina, lat. 159, fols. 3 and 4.

716 and 717. Niccolò da Bologna: *February*. *January* (fire repainted). Munich, Bayr. Staatsbibliothek, lat. 10072, fols. 2v and 2.

718. Associate of Brussels Initials Master:
January. London, Brit. Mus., Add. 29433, fol. 1.

719. Brussels Initials Master: *January*.
Warsaw, Bibl. Narodowa, lat. Q.v.I.111, fol. 2.

724. Brussels Initials Workshop: *April*. Oxford, Bodl. Lib., Douce 62, fol. 6.

725. Brussels Initials Workshop: *May*. Oxford, Bodl. Lib., Douce 62, fol. 7.

726. Brussels Initials Workshop: *May*. London, Brit. Mus., Add. 29433, fol. 5.

720–723. Brussels Initials Master: *February. March. April. October*. Warsaw, Bibl. Narodowa, lat. Q.v.I.111, fols. 2v, 3, 3v, 6v.

727 and 728. Brussels Initials Master: *St. Luke. St. Matthew*. Parma, Bibl. Palatina, lat. 159, fols. 15v and 17v.

729 and 730. Brussels Initials Master: *St. Matthew. St. Luke*. Cleveland, Museum of Art, *Heures de Charles le Noble*, pp. 49 and 45.

731. Brussels Initials Master: *St. Mark*.
Cleveland, Museum of Art, *Heures de Charles le Noble*, p. 53.

732. Turone, 1360: *Evangelist* (detail of altarpiece).
Verona, Castelvecchio.

733. Brussels Initials Master: *St. Mark*.
London, Brit. Mus., Add. 29433, fol. 16v.

734. Brussels Initials Master: *St. John*.
Cleveland, Museum of Art, *Heures de Charles le Noble*, p. 42.

735 and 736. Follower of Jacquemart: *Annunciation. Annunciation to the Shepherds.* Parma, Bibl. Palatina, lat. 159, fols. 22 and 56.

737 and 738. Follower of Jacquemart: *Visitation. Adoration of the Magi.* Parma, Bibl. Palatina, lat. 159, fols. 35 and 62.

739 and 740. French, *ca.* 1402: *Visitation. Nativity.* Oxford, Bodl. Lib., Douce 62, fols. 51v and 63.

741. Luçon Workshop: *St. Christopher.*
London, Brit. Mus., Add. 29433, fol. 205.

742. Luçon Workshop: *Madonna* (retouched).
Oxford, Bodl. Lib., Douce 62, fol. 171v.

743. French Master: *Coronation of the Virgin.*
London, Brit. Mus., Add. 29433, fol. 83.

744. Altichiero: *Martyrdom of St. Lucy* (detail).
Padua, S. Giorgio.

745. Brussels Initials Master: *Annunciation*.
Cleveland, Museum of Art, *Heures de Charles le Noble*, p. 57.

746. The Limbourgs: *St. Catherine*.
New York, The Cloisters, *Belles Heures*, fol. 15.

747. Brussels Initials Master: *Annunciation*.
London, Brit. Mus., Add. 29433, fol. 20.

748. Brussels Initials Master: *Visitation.*
Madrid, Bibl. del Palacio, ms. 2099, fol. 51.

749. Brussels Initials Master: *Visitation.*
Cleveland, Museum of Art, *Heures de Charles le Noble*, p. 109.

750. Brussels Initials Master: *Visitation.*
London, Brit. Mus., Add. 29433, fol. 43v.

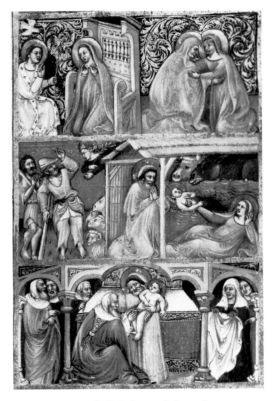

751. Niccolò da Bologna: Infancy Scenes.
Munich, Bayr. Staatsbibliothek, lat. 10072, fol. 160v.

752. Brussels Initials Master: *Nativity*. Madrid, Bibl. del Palacio, ms. 2099, fol. 62.

753. Brussels Initials Workshop: *Adoration of the Magi*. Oxford, Bodl. Lib., Douce 62, fol. 73v.

755. Brussels Initials Master: *Nativity*. London, Brit. Mus., Add. 29433, fol. 56.

754. Brussels Initials Master: *Adoration of the Magi*. Madrid, Bibl. del Palacio, ms. 2099, fol. 72v.

756. Pisan, *ca.* 1400: *Nativity with St. Bridget.* Pisa, Museo Civico.

757. Piero della Francesca: *St. Joseph* (detail of *Nativity*).
London, National Gallery.

758. Brussels Initials Master: *Nativity.* Cleveland,
Museum of Art, *Heures de Charles le Noble*, p. 133.

760. Brussels Initials Workshop: *Adoration of the Magi*.
London, Brit. Mus., Add. 29433, fol. 67.

759. Brussels Initials Master: *Adoration of the Magi*.
Cleveland, Museum of Art, *Heures de Charles le Noble*, p. 156.

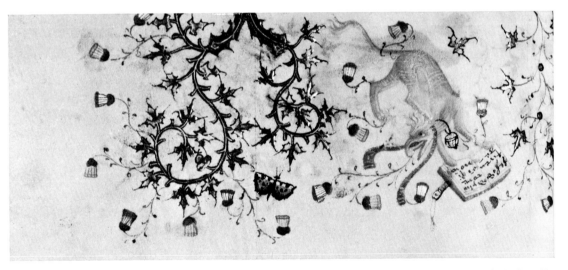

761. Associate of Brussels Initials Master: *Monster Holding Inscribed Book*. Cleveland, Museum of Art, *Heures de Charles le Noble*, p. 414.

762. Brussels Initials Workshop: *A Strange Barbecue*. London, Brit. Mus., Add. 29433, fol. 59.

763. Brussels Initials Master: *Flight into Egypt.*
Madrid, Bibl. del Palacio, ms. 2099, fol. 81v.

764. Brussels Initials Master: *Flight into Egypt.*
Cleveland, Museum of Art, *Heures de Charles le Noble*, p. 175.

765. Brussels Initials Master: *Flight into Egypt.*
London, Brit. Mus., Add. 29433, fol. 76.

766. South French: *Flight into Egypt.*
London, Brit. Mus., Harley 2979, fol. 54.

767. Brussels Initials Master: *Flight into Egypt*.
Oxford, Bodl. Lib., Douce 62, fol. 82v.

768. Brussels Initials Workshop: *Annunciation to the Shepherds*.
Madrid, Bibl. del Palacio, ms. 2099, fol. 68.

769. Brussels Initials Master: *Trinity*.
London, Brit. Mus., Add. 29433, fol. 192.

770. Brussels Initials Master: *Coronation of the Virgin*.
Madrid, Bibl. del Palacio, ms. 2099, fol. 88v.

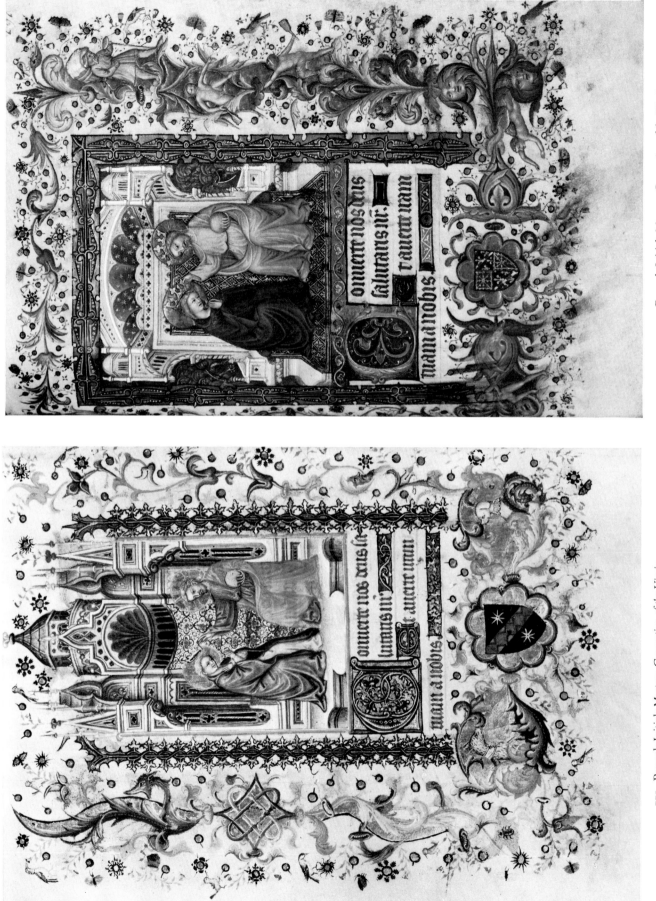

772. Brussels Initials Master: *Coronation of the Virgin.*
Cleveland, Museum of Art, *Heures de Charles le Noble*, p. 191.

771. Brussels Initials Master: *Coronation of the Virgin.*
Oxford, Bodl. Lib., Douce 62, fol. 89v.

773. Altichiero: *Coronation of the Virgin* (detail). Padua, S. Giorgio.

774. Altichiero: *Coronation of the Virgin* (detail). Padua, Eremitani (destroyed).

789. Brussels Initials Master: *Hell*. Cleveland, Museum of Art, *Heures de Charles le Noble*, p. 211.

790. Brussels Initials Master: *Hell*. London, Brit. Mus., Add. 29433, fol. 89.

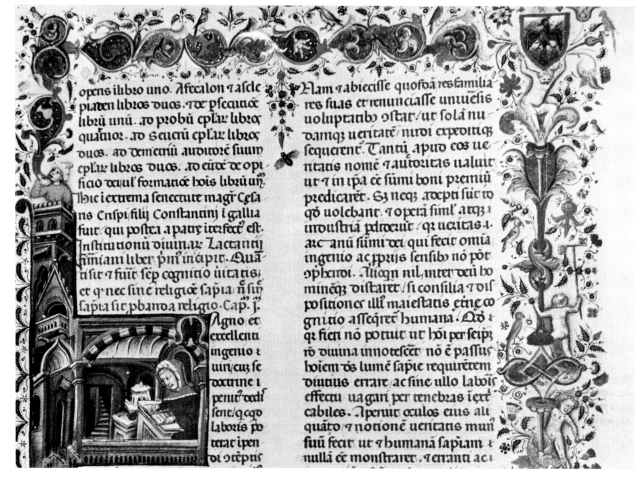

791. Brussels Initials Workshop: Lactantius, Bk. I. Holkham Hall, ms. 120, fol. 2.

792. Brussels Initials Master, 1408: *Madonna and Battuti*.
Bologna, Archiginnasio, *Statuti della Compagnia dello Spedale di S. Maria della Vita*.

794. Brussels Initials Workshop: *Constantine*.
Holkham Hall, ms. 120, fol. 84v.

793. Italian associate of Brussels Initials Master:
Priest Blessing the Host. Holkham Hall, ms. 120, fol. 103.

795. Brussels Initials Workshop (?): *St. Catherine*.
Modena, Bibl. Estense, lat. 1021, fol. 195.

796. Brussels Initials Workshop: *A Prophet*.
Venice, Fondazione Cini.

797. Brussels Initials Workshop: *St. Dominic*. Whereabouts unknown.

798. Brussels Initials Master: *Holy Family*.
Madrid, Bibl. del Palacio, ms. 2099, fol. 166v.

799. Brussels Initials Master: *Fontaine de Tous Biens*.
London, Brit. Mus., Add. 29433, fol. 168.

800 and 801. Bolognese (Brussels Initials Master?): *Hell. Birth of the Virgin*. London, Brit. Mus., Add. 34247, fols. 85 and 45v.

802. Bolognese, *ca.* 1356: *A Court of Justice.*
Vienna, Nationalbibliothek, ms. 2048–9, fol. 149.

803. Veronese: *Temptation of Christ.*
Verona, Bibl. Capitolare, Cor. 5, fol. 95.

804. Follower of Master of Berry's Cleres Femmes: *Way to Calvary.*
Cleveland, Museum of Art, *Heures de Charles le Noble*, p. 355.

805. Egerton Master: *Entombment.*
Cleveland, Museum of Art, *Heures de Charles le Noble*, p. 405.

806. Brussels Initials Workshop: *Man of Sorrows*.
London, Brit. Mus., Add. 29433, fol. 107v.

807. Jacques Daliwe: *Man of Sorrows*.
Berlin, Preussische Staatsbibliothek (formerly).

808. Brussels Initials Master: *Man of Sorrows*.
Madrid, Bibl. del Palacio, ms. 2099, fol. 172v.

809. Brussels Initials Master: *Man of Sorrows*.
Cleveland, Museum of Art, *Heures de Charles le Noble*, p. 255.

810. Luçon Master, 1401: *Man of Sorrows.*
Barcelona, Bibl. Central, ms. 1850, fol. 177v.

811. Brussels Initials Master: *Vesperbild.*
London, Brit. Mus., Add. 29433, fol. 174.

812. Brussels Initials Master: *Crucifixion.*
Cleveland, Museum of Art, *Heures de Charles le Noble*, p. 379.

813. Egerton Master: *Deposition.*
Cleveland, Museum of Art, *Heures de Charles le Noble*, p. 395.

814. Romanesque: The Altar of Aracoeli. Rome, S. Maria in Aracoeli.

815. Italian, 1285: *Legend of Aracoeli.* Modena, Bibl. Estense, lat. 461, fol. 92v.

816. German, 14th century: *Legend of Aracoeli.* London, Brit. Mus., Add. 38119, fol. 29.

817. Egerton Master: *Legend of Aracoeli.* Paris, Bibl. nat., fr. 606, fol. 46.

819. Roman, *ca.* 1300: *Madonna and Two Angels*. Rome, S. Maria in Aracoeli.

818. Niccolò da Bologna: *Legend of Aracoeli*.
Rome, Bibl. Vaticana, lat. 2639, fol. 2v.

821. Gentile da Fabriano: *Madonna*. Pisa, Museo Civico.

820. Venetian, *ca.* 1390: *Legend of Aracoeli*. Stuttgart, Württembergische Staatsgalerie.

822. Master of the *Coronation*: *St. Matthew*.
Paris, Bibl. nat., fr. 159, fol. 426.

823. Master of the Coronation (?), 1402: *Man of Sorrows*.
New York, Morgan Library, ms. 515, fol. 130v.

824. Master of Berry's Cleres Femmes, before 1405: *Crucifixion*.
Paris, Bibl. nat., fr. 120, fol. 520.

825. Master of Berry's Cleres Femmes: Livy III, 3.
Geneva, Bibl. publique et universitaire, fr. 77, fol. 356.

· Mercurius · ☿

826 and 827. Bruges, before 1403: *Mercury. Moon in Exaltation*. New York, Morgan Library, ms. 785, fols. 47 and 50v.

828. Flemish: *Way to Calvary*.
Brussels, Bibl. royale, ms. 10176–8, fol. 275v.

829. Master of Berry's Cleres Femmes, *ca.* 1405:
Jews before Pharaoh. Paris, Bibl. de l'Arsenal, ms. 5057, fol. 44.

830. Jean de Beaumetz: *Madonnas*. Basel, Öffentliche Kunstsammlung, Kupferstichkabinett.

831. Jean de Beaumetz: *Crucifixion*. Cleveland, Museum of Art.

832. Malouel: *Trinity with Man of Sorrows*. Paris, Louvre.

833 and 834. Epître Master: *Atropos and her Victims. Latona and the Frogs.* Paris, Bibl. nat., fr. 606, fols. 17 and 11 v.

835 and 836. Épître Master: *Fortune. A Siege.* Chantilly, Musée Condé, ms. 494, fols. 16 and 70.

837. Bolognese, *ca.* 1310: *Esdras*, II. Gerona, Cathedral, Bible of Jean de Berry.

838. Copy of a Parisian *joyau, ca.* 1404.
Munich, Bayrisches Nationalmuseum.

839. The Passion Master: *St. Michael.*
Paris, Bibl. nat., lat. 1052, fol. 519.

840. Style of Pseudo-Jacquemart: *Angel.*
Paris, Coll. Jean Lafond.

841. Virgil Master, 1403: *Virgil's Georgics.*
Florence, Bibl. Laurenziana, Med. Pal. 69, fol. 18.

842. French: Reverse of Reliquary of Jean de Berry. London, Brit. Mus.

843. Master of Berry Apocalypse: *God, Adam and Eve*. New York, Morgan Library, ms. 133, fol. 81 v.

844. The Limbourgs: *October*. Chantilly, Musée Condé, *Très Riches Heures*, fol. 10v.

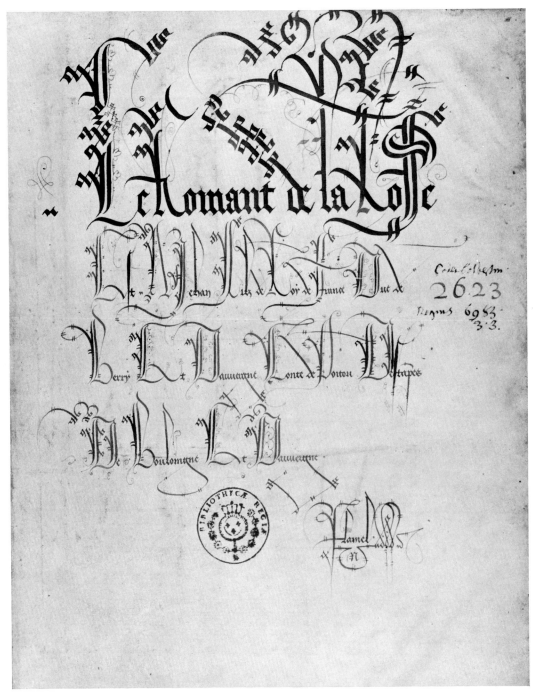

845. *Ex libris* of Jean de Berry written by Jean Flamel, 1403. Paris, Bibl. nat., fr. 380, fol. A.

LIST OF ILLUSTRATIONS

LIST OF ILLUSTRATIONS

The author and the publishers are grateful to all institutions, collectors and photographers who have supplied photographs for reproduction in this volume. The negatives of those photographs supplied by the author himself will be given to the Archive of the Bibliothèque Nationale in Paris.